HOW LITTLE WE ARE

A Collection Of Thoughts

NEWTON C. JIBUNOH

HOW LITTLE WE ARE

A Collection Of Thoughts

FOREWORD BY
WOLE SOYINKA

PYXIDIA HOUSE PUBLISHERS

HOW LITTLE WE ARE - A Collection Of Thoughts

Request for information on this title should be addressed to

Newton C. Jibunoh

Didi Museum, Akin Adesola Str, Victoria Island, Lagos, Nigeria
Email: fadeafrica@yahoo.co.uk

Library of Congress Cataloging-in-Publication Data

Newton C. Jibunoh
HOW LITTLE WE ARE - A Collection Of Thoughts
ISBN-13: 978-1-946530-21-9 (Paperback)
ISBN-10: 1-946530-21-2 (Paperback)
1. Economic - Environment - Nonfiction 1. Title
Library of Congress Control Number: 2020931884

Edited by Winnie Aduayi
Cover Design by Rick Hughes

Published in Dallas Texas by Pyxidia House Publishers. A registered trademark of Pyxidia Concept llc. www.pyxidiahouse.com
info@pyxidiahouse.com

Printed in the United States of America

To the younger generation who have the immense responsibility of repairing the damage caused by my generation.

AKNOWLEDGEMENT

Growing up in the village, the appearance of the full moon always led to one of the most exciting gatherings of children because of the storytelling from explorers, hunters and fishermen. As children, we were told stories about the rivers, forests, and even things created by nature that the ordinary eyes could not see. Their exploits shaped my early life, and though I no longer remember their names, their stories remain with me. As I put together this collection of thoughts, I remain eternally grateful to them.

The journey to publishing my fourth book started with a home visit by two former governors, Governor Emmanuel Uduagha and Governor Orji Uzor Kalu on my 80th birthday. The killing fields of Benue by the Fulani herdsmen was a very topical issue at that time, and the fact that I had predicted the crisis over 20years ago dominated our conversation. What started as a friendly encounter with old acquaintances led to the start of my weekly column with the Sun Newspaper as the two governors, one of which was the owner of the said newspaper, pleaded with me to share more thought with more people. I eventually agreed, and this opened a gap for me that has widened over the years. At first, it was a weekly column for a few weeks; then a few months, and now, it's been over two years, and I'm still writing after over a hundred articles, some of which is now featured in this book.

All the writings and research wouldn't have been possible without some of my colleagues at Fight Against Desert Encroachment (FADE) Africa. I would like to express my gratitude to Onuorah Aligbe who often researched and contributed from Atlanta, USA. He also accompanied me on my fourth desert expedition. Bunmi Obanawu, who travelled with me extensively and proofread almost all hundred articles published in the Sun Newspaper. Abdulazeez Abba, who helped with some research from Kano and is also a member of the board of FADE. And Ambassador Ayo Olukanni, who is the Vice president of FADE Africa and was also part of the mission control during my third desert expedition to the Sahara. I also acknowledge the contribution of Akin Olukiran, who was FADE's representative in London from inception. Dr. Dike Okwuelum, and FADE's most recent addition, Chiamaka.

Of course, I can't do without appreciating members of my family that have made contributions - Didi Jibunoh and Ceejay Jibunoh. The re-workings and making of the articles into a book was made possible by Winnie Aduayi, the Editor, Pyxidia House Publishers, Dallas, USA.

Finally, I would like to appreciate Wole Soyinka whom I met decades ago, during the preparation of Festac '77 and have remained friends with him ever since for writing the foreword. Every time I think of Wole Soyinka and his works, particularly poetry, I remember the likes of Mozart, Tchaikovsky and Beethoven.

CONTENTS

PART III - CORRUPTION

PART IV - LEADERSHIP AND POWER

PART V – THE HERDSMEN SAGA

PART VI – THE ENVIRONMENT

PART VII – THE LOSSES

PART VIII - THE RESONATORS

FOREWORD

It is over three decades now that I found myself bombarded by calls from an acquaintance, from my own portion of the country, who insisted that he must see me urgently. He was a lawyer, had attained the status of SAN, enjoyed a high professional regard from the public, and even more importantly, from among his own peers. We were of the same generation; he was just a few years older. He needed to see me on a matter that troubled him, one that he felt was right "up your street". I have completely forgotten the actual nature of the problem, but it had come to his notice through his legal practice and involved a familiar national malaise.

We met, he outlined the issue; it really is frustrating that I can no longer recall what it was, all such details being obliterated, not merely by ageing memory, but by the finality of the exchange that followed. That exchange ended up supplanting the originating

issue. What happened was that, as he rose to take his leave, I said, "But what about you?"
He stopped, looked at me askance and queried, "What about me?"
"Yes, you. You have a voice, a public voice. You even have forensic credentials. You have a direct, first-hand knowledge of this problem. So, don't you think you are in the best position to bring this to both government and public attention? It is, after all, of public interest."

Impossible ever to forget his reaction. His countenance changed instantly. He drew himself straight up to his dignified height, head thrown back, his eyes blazing as if to transfix a witness under cross-examination, perhaps a juicy human morsel trapped into committing a perjury as he delivered the coup de grace:
"I never engage in public controversy."

And that of course, was the end of the matter. He never again attempted to saddle me with any undertaking that offended the dignity of his calling or social status, and we retained an even relationship of friendly interaction until his demise some years ago.

It is therefore with a genuine heave of satisfaction that I occasionally encounter manuscripts from concerned individuals outside the familiar clutch of "professional agitators", those exceptions who feel sufficiently impassioned on any social issue to set aside time from routine preoccupations and address their public directly from an informed position. When their credentials also include action taken on behalf of those "coming-out" issues – that is, embossed with the ancient adage "action speaks louder than words", then of course, one feels a personal sense of solidarity, and even obligation, to call attention to their efforts to communicate those concerns with the public. After a while, the accustomed interventionists become predictable, their voices jaded, and begin to lose impact. Their collective effort benefits from the injection of new points of view from unfamiliar directions. This has the effect of checking a complacent public in stride, struck by a convergence of concerns from a variety of interests and directions over issues that have only silently agitated them.

Invitation to contribute a word to this collection of thoughts also offered me an opportunity to pay a long missing personal tribute to one of the true heroes of my generation. This was a man, who, quite early in life, crossed the Sahara Desert solo, not even once but – TWICE! When his 'fellow conspirators' dropped out of the original venture, he took on the collective challenge and proceeded on his own. Now that, in my view, is an expression of will-power and tenacity that has become exceedingly rare in this society. Spurred by nothing more than a spirit of adventure, he embraced the formidable risks in which survival was often at the sheer whim of providence. Yet, he returned to the fray one more time, this time to learn more about the enemy and engineer its defeat. From those "madcap" voyages, Newton Jibunoh developed a very special, personal, indeed spiritual relationship with the desert. From a straightforward response to its mystical immensity; however, he brought himself down to earth in grasping its implications for the survival of his immediate humanity.

Again, he did not let this awareness remain in the domain of words alone – he acted. He set up, and empowered an organization, FADE, dedicated to stemming the Sahara tide of encroachment and ameliorate its impact on the human habitat. Like Mathaai Wangari of Kenya and her dedicated women, he has planted millions of trees. He set up programmes, personally led the charge against desertification. While avoiding the tendency to reduce the human predatory malice in the present violence inflicted on Nigerians by nomadic herdsmen, he takes time to call our attention to the fact that failure to deal with a Nature threat should be factored into a holistic response to a menace that is now accurately reckoned to be more deadly to Nigerians and neigbouring nations than the insurgency of Boko Haram, among other plagues on the survival of nations.

The new tide of migration – unemployment, internecine wars of increasing intensity – also owes much to failure to confront Nature well in advance of her own onslaught on human complacency. The especial value of interjections of such aroused voices and consciences as Newton Jibunoh is quite simple: if one man has sufficient resolve to conquer the desert, what excuse do governments have? And indeed, the rest of us? The very puny stature of man faced with the might of Nature has proved, paradoxically, the very spur to his giant achievements in bringing that same Nature under human control. This is the thrust, and challenge, of Jibunoh's musings.

Wole Soyinka

PREFACE

The idea for this book arose in 2018 out of a pair of firm convictions. The first was that the political emancipation we had all been expecting immensely for more than two decades was as riveting a spectacle as modern politics had ever produced. The second was that much of the reality of the political, economic, and environmental situation of Nigeria had not been told. What is missing and might be of enduring value is an intimate portrait of the fragility of our nation, Nigeria.

Most of the crisis that are with us today started two to three decades ago and I predicted them: the climate crisis, the food insecurity, the killing fields everywhere, unemployment and adverse poverty, the disappearing grazing fields and the drying up of the Lake Chad, and the political rascality. All these could have been avoided with the much-anticipated leadership. It was, therefore, by chance that I shared my fears over the fragility of our nation with two past governors when they paid me a visit on my 80th birthday and it led to a prompt for me to share more of my thoughts with the world. That was when the novelty of writing a weekly column in the national newspaper, The Sun, started.

What we do and don't do is essential. Everything rises and falls on these; it all matters. The attitude of the citizens, the cunning of political players, the economic ticking time bomb, the killing and kidnapping fields, the dependence and dominance of Oil. The elegance of nature, the warnings of the environment, the dare of the Sahara and its shifting dunes. The dangers of the advancing beaches, the broken breaches and the collapsing federal and state infrastructures. The abuse of power, the difference between historical guilt and historical responsibility, loss of monumental artefacts, and the follies of idle young minds.

These are the things that most engage me. They fill my days, and some trouble my nights. They give me pause, pain, pleasure, wonder. And for six decades, they have occupied my mind and commanded my pen. These things may not matter to everyone, but it should, for our existence as a people largely depends on them. I have driven through the Sahara four times; twice alone from London to Nigeria and Nigeria to London; and twice with a group of young men and women, witnessing firsthand while seeking solutions to the dangerous advancement of the desert into habitable communities and displacing such communities.

Having had over four decades of a successful career as a building engineer, one would think I would spend my days enjoying the best of retirement, but I firmly believe that what moves a man, what elevates the mind, what makes us fully human are all these things that lie beyond one's personal comfort. We can have the best cultural efflorescence and life, but if we get the environment and politics wrong, everything stands to be swept away; more particularly politics - groups of people organized to gain and exercise power, which so far in its conduct in Nigeria has been immensely abused. Thus, I dare say, in the end, our personal comfort and selfishness must bow to the sovereignty of nationhood if we must continue to have a nation to call ours.

One of the most universal cravings of our time is a hunger for compelling and resourceful leaders. Some of us spent our early years in the eras of such great leaders like Mahatma Gandhi and Nelson Mandela. These giants strode across our cultural, intellectual and political horizons. Their followers everywhere marched with them, fought with them, and some died for their quest for the betterment of governance and humanity; these leaders could not be ignored.

Today, rather than this life and death engagement with true leadership birthing more like-minded leaders, the selfish few who wield much power has used the same engagement to make way for the cult of personal interest while riding on the coattail of "the government of the people for the people." The crisis of our nation today is the mediocrity and irresponsibility of so many of the men and women in power and those who back them. We fail to grasp the essence of leadership that is relevant to these times of environmental and socio-economic decline, and hence, we cannot agree even on the standards by which to measure, vote, appoint and reject. Does it matter that we lack these standards? Absolutely! Without guiding standards and considered practical experiences, we continue to lack the very foundation for knowledge of good leadership that touches and shapes a great nation; without such standards, we cannot make vital distinctions between good and corrupt leaders; we cannot distinguish leaders from power wielders and despots. A leader and a power wielder are polar opposites. Nelson Mandela was a leader. Thus, this begs the question, would we ever find another

Mandela for Africa, and especially for our nation, Nigeria?

We must understand that nationhood is nothing, if not linked to collective purpose, and that the effectiveness of our leaders must be judged not by their well-manicured political press image but by actual social change measured by intent and the satisfaction of the people's needs and expectations. We must understand that our political leadership depends on a chain of processes; of the interplay between the calls of moral principles and the recognized necessities of power. We must also understand that in placing these concepts of political leadership centrally into a supposition of historical causation, we will affirm the possibilities of the human volition and prevailing standards of justice in the conduct of the people's affairs.

Life in the corridors of power is a never-ending game that requires constant vigilance and tactile thinking of the people being ruled. It's a civilized war. Therefore we, the people, must begin to think and ask pertinent questions. By so doing, we spare ourselves and the younger generation the pain that comes from playing with fire without knowing its properties.

PART I

THE NATION, NIGERIA

"No nation can ever hold up its head, far less take pride of place amongst the nations of the world if the individuals of which it is comprised think of nothing but personal gain and self-glorification."

— Maulana Wahiduddin Khan

Nigeria:
A Fractured Nation

The saying that one cannot eat one's cake and have it may be lost on our nation, Nigeria. For it appears that we eat the nation's cake and still manage to share it at the same time. Our government seems to lack any sense of accountability to the citizens on how our resources are applied, which is further exacerbated by overpopulation. It is worrisome that we have not been able to explain how the country's population went from six million at Independence to close to 150 million in the year 2000 despite the huge amount of money that has been invested in population commissions. It is a known fact that the Nigerian borders are so porous coupled with inadequate security; thus, migrants from such countries like Cameroun, Niger, Chad, and the Republic of Benin, pour into Nigeria in their millions and do not return to their countries, further stretching our resources thin. This phenomenon has bloated our population so much so that we cannot keep up with the census, but rather give estimates that are frequently being revised. This is bad for socio-economic planning. It is bad politics, and it breeds courtship with danger. One of the projects the massive funding of the Population Commission was used for about 20 years ago, was the 'Identity Card' project, which was meant to accurately document and identify actual citizens and legal residents of Nigeria in order to better serve and enrich the lives of the people. Till date, we are yet to catalogue every citizen and give each an ID card. This is a cause of grave concern, even more so, as it leaves unchecked room for the continued decline in all facets of the nation.

I once read a statement in an opinion piece of a daily newspaper, and it has stuck with me ever since: "Love for one's country is a primordial affection that does not hinge basically on anything substantial, simply an intangible essence with no physical substance, yet vicariously glorious."

In that article, the writer was asking if Nigeria deserved our patriotism. He explained that over the years, Nigeria had had a deficient and decadent political class and leadership elite that robbed the nation of its well-deserved chance to sport among its peers and superiors as an eminent member of the comity of nations, both in terms of development and prosperity for its citizens. In other words, Nigeria was like a ship that has been steered for so long by captains who are either grossly inept at steering or are selfishly setting a course that benefited only self. It makes one wonder just when the right time is to abandon the ship.

One thing that rings true in all the different scenarios and challenges Nigeria is faced with is the lack of patriotism that abounds in the country because only one who cares nothing for his or her nation will work tireless to destroy it like so many of our leaders and even the rest of us do. I recall an incident that happened during a visit to Accra, Ghana, and how I witnessed a citizen arrest at work. It all happened when a taxi driver lost control of his car and ran into a cable pole by the roadside. The impact caused the pole to come down. Immediately, people gathered around, and members of the public arrested the taxi driver before the arrival of the police. Now, this is very different from mob justice, which is against the law of the land and humanity. The driver wasn't assaulted but made to stay put until the police arrived.

The main lesson for me here was the respect people had for public property. As far as the people were concerned, the cable pole belonged to everyone, and so they had a responsibility to safeguard it, or like in this case, ensure that the situation was adequately attended to and managed. Here in Nigeria, the taxi driver would have been on his merry way because as long as it is for the 'government', no one cares. Worse still, if the knocked-down cable pole hurt anyone around there, jungle justice would have been carried out immediately, where the taxi driver would have been lynched. Most of us lack a sense of belonging, and it is not easy to be patriotic when you don't belong.

Sadly, these monumental and grave challenges that Nigeria is faced with have been with us for decades. And unless the leaders and those that are led can demonstrate some love for the nation, Nigeria will continue in crisis. And this crisis brings with it disjointed development, massive corruption, civil war everywhere and anywhere, deficiency in educational and health development, infrastructural decay, and everybody to himself or herself position. There is no more love for the nation anywhere, which is known as patriotism. So, let me begin by trying to explain what patriotism is and what it means to a nation like Nigeria.

In the 2000s, a particular part of the nation wanted

and went as far as instituting Sharia law in some states; about nine of them. However, rather than examine and try to understand the reason behind this, we swept everything under the carpet, ignored the situation and continued with our lives. My understanding then was that a good part of Nigeria was no longer happy with western education and lifestyle. It is possible that this activism went underground and came out as Boko Haram. The same can be said for when the advocacy for resource control started in the South-South of Nigeria. We can see what the result of that unaddressed agitation is now.

When we hear the word patriotism, we think it's all about laying down our lives for the country. I beg to differ as I would describe Patriotism as intense loyalty to one's nation and its interest. It is a well-known fact that most of the developed countries of the world today attained greatness, partly as a result of the patriotism shown by their citizens. From the kneeling movement in America to the Biafra protests in Nigeria, people have come up with different ways of expressing their discontent with society. We have instances where tribes rebel against the government for being excluded from the government and societal benefits. If we look at the recent issues with regards to the Niger-Delta militants and the Biafran movement, there's a common lack of patriotism, which in turn causes a backlash from the government. For the Niger-Deltans who harbour the majority of the country's oil, yet live in dire poverty, is their lack of patriotism justified?

Again, as with the case of the Sharia states, there was no concerted effort to sit down and discuss their advocacy. If you put these scenarios together, you will see that majority of Nigerians don't feel any sense of belonging to their nation. It is impossible to be patriotic when you don't belong. Particularly, the unorganized and politically oriented ruling class that does not understand democracy has helped in sweeping the problem to promote their selfish agenda. Even when the faith and traditional institutions in the country tried to mediate in many instances, they were sidelined. So, what we have now is that the carpet has been turned over and the dirt is now hunting and killing us.

Lack of Patriotism cuts across, tribe, religion, age, and status, and that is the reason you see the Igbos queue behind and defend a national thief who is an Igbo man; the Hausas and Yorubas do the same when someone from their tribe is caught stealing the nation's resources. It is not only with the leaders, but the followers as well. Patriotic followers can check the excesses of unpatriotic leaders, but in the Nigerian situation, the followers turn a blind eye and claim to mind their own business; funny when they usually aren't known for minding their own business.

True Patriotism, not a lack of it, will make it hard for an individual to embezzle funds meant to provide health facilities for 170 million Nigerians. A lack of Patriotism is the reason why an individual will embezzle billions of naira meant for the construction of Federal and State roads. It is a lack of patriotism that will make an individual embezzle billions meant to improve our aviation industry and allow Nigerians to fly in rickety aircraft from sub-standard airports waiting for death. It is lack of patriotism that makes an individual or groups spend huge sums of money that can be used to better the lives of Nigerians to sponsor terrorists and militants to kill and make life uncomfortable for Nigerians. It is lack of patriotism that makes a public officer embezzle billions meant to improve the education sector and instead send his or her family members abroad to study. It is lack of patriotism that makes an individual embezzle billions of dollars meant to improve power supply, leaving millions of Nigerians in darkness. The list goes on, but it doesn't just stop with the ones with the power and opportunity because it is lack of patriotism that makes an average Nigerian watch with indifference and docility while a few embezzle the national resources and wreck the country.

I can only imagine that those who fought and died to put this country together are now spitting at us from their graves for making a mockery of their gallantry, and as such it appears that nobody is prepared to die again for Nigeria. And it boils down to everybody for themselves, everybody sharing and eating the national cake together until it is all finished. Will the cake finish before the sharing or will the sharing finish before the cake? I highly doubt the latter and seriously fear the former.

A Fractured Nation: Patriotism

A few years ago, I was invited by Nnamdi Azikiwe University to deliver the Annual lecture with the theme, "Environmental Management and Conservation" but was asked by the University to pick my related topic and so I decided on *"Land Is Life"*. The lecture was subsequently published, and when my son read the publication, he was fascinated because his son, my 8th grandchild's, name is Anibundu, which means *land is life*. In the publication, I had discussed the land of our nation in details; the air we breathe, the food we eat and the water we drink - the three most important components of life that come from the land, and of course, we return to the land when we die. I also discussed the need to respect and give back to the land as much as we have taken, even possibly more, so that we can leave the land a better place than we met it. This part of the lecture invoked a lot of conversations, questions and answers between my son and me. The part that was of much interest to him was leaving the land a better place than we met it. He felt that with so much political instability, disjointed economic plans, destruction of the environment, and the seeming threats all over the country that it would take a lot to bring the land and its people back to normalcy. I agreed with him but told him that since we are still on this land that we may be able to put things right before departing this land. However, he wondered how long it would take to stop the insurgencies, militancy, herdsmen crisis, and the monumental corruption, which is currently affecting development.

To this, I pointed out that the quickest way to bring back Nigeria to the one nation it once was, is to bring back PATRIOTISM. Nigerians no longer belong to Nigeria and we must find a way of giving Nigerians some sense of belonging, something to fight for like HOPE, but not false hope. Security not amnesty; Opportunity to quality education, not contracts or appointments; Justice, not politics without defined ideologies. Nigerians know how to go from poverty to wealth despite the huge disadvantages in our economy. Nigerians also know how to handle ill health to good health without having to travel abroad for medicals. My son would like to be able to work in every part of Nigeria the way I did. I told him that it is possible, but again we must first bring back PATRIOTISM by going back to those things that united us, not the senseless political divisions, senseless religious ideologies and senseless ethnic boundaries that never existed but were created by men and women of fortune for selfish gratification.

Let's start by looking at sports. In my days, we had national sports competitions in schools and colleges. Nigeria's young college students travelled all over the country to compete, from that level, we were able to develop athletes who trained on our land and competed abroad. Today, they train abroad and compete abroad. We had the National and West African Sports Festivals, and three major stadiums that were built to international standard in Lagos, Ibadan and Kaduna. The Festivals were something the young all over the country looked forward to. Notable international athletes came to Nigeria to compete. The whole nation came together because it was beholding to belong. We saw recently how children of immigrants won the World Cup; the whole of France forgot that the majority of their players were blacks and that the far right didn't even want blacks in France. When Nigeria played in the recently concluded World Cup, as I drove past some grazing fields in my state, Delta, I saw some Fulani herdsmen clutching to their telephones and transistor radios rooting for Nigeria. I was also told that Boko Haram members were rooting for Nigeria and that the militants in the creeks had a more sophisticated satellite system which enabled them to watch all the matches. So why is the Unity of Nigeria going the wrong way? Why is it that we cannot explore the unifying spirit of sports to bring our nation together again?

Another way of unifying the nation is through Art. I remember the World Festival of Arts hosted by Nigeria in 1977. It took the country almost 18 months to prepare; the whole nation was agog with preparations leading to the main festival. Most Nigerians did not realise how rich and powerful Nigerian Arts and Culture was until FESTAC '77. Before then Nigerians imported Lilies, landscape paintings and drawings from Europe and Asia to decorate their homes and offices. But from FESTAC '77 till date, most homes and offices and public spaces are now decorated with Nigerian Art. It also became known that West African Art influenced artists like Matisse and Picasso. FESTAC '77 also made us realise that Nigeria was the third largest owner of Nigerian Arts abroad because while we were importing foreign art, foreigners and expatriates were carting away Nigerian Art. FESTAC '77 gave us Festac Town and National Theatre. FESTAC '77 brought Nigerians together not only for Nigerians but to showcase Nigeria to the rest of the world.

We didn't develop on the novelty of FESTAC '77 delivered to us, like many other things, we turned our back on it. It almost feels like every time we are on the verge of something good, we self-sabotage it. The way things are today, most Nigerians feel that there is nothing to fight for and that their voices are never heard. The security agencies and the judicial system that are meant to defend and protect the rights of the citizens are never there for them.

Thus, patriotism must be seen from the standpoint of every Nigerian belonging to Nigeria. The nation has gone through senseless wars, misrule, and leadership deficits, insurgencies and political racialism. These issues cannot be corrected or rebuilt in four or eight years, especially when those years still dwell in the bossom of sycophancy and incompetency. We must, therefore, seek leadership that can bring everybody together during these difficult times. That kind of leadership is one that doesn't colour within the tribal lines but provides the necessary infrastructure for all tribes. The type of leadership that can be held accountable for wrongdoing without blaming past administrations or everybody else. A leadership that eschews corruption by surrounding itself with people who have the appropriate skill set and not people with pending court cases of wrongdoing whether 'proven' or not. The list is endless, but it is useless if we, the people, don't demand it by seeking it out while neglecting the rest. Only then can we be able to build a nation where peace and justice shall reign as contained in the last paragraph of our National Anthem.

Policing (Or Lack Of) and Nigeria

One evening, during a recent festive period in my hometown, I decided to visit a friend in the neighbouring town, and as is customary for me in my hometown, I drove myself. All over my state, I happen to be known as the Desert Warrior. So, as I drove to my destination, I came upon a Police Checkpoint, where about four policemen were stationed. As soon as they noticed me, they began chanting, *"Desert Warrior, your boys are here."* It was the festive period, so I chose to pull over, and as I did, one of them ran over, and I gave him N2000 for all of them. Immediately I did, he put one of the notes into his pocket and held up the other shouting to his colleagues that the Desert warrior has given them N1000. I almost reversed to challenge him, but he was carrying a gun, and I didn't want to be the victim of an accidental discharge.

This only goes to show just how corrupt the average policeman is, even to his fellow mates. So how far down can we go before something is done to check the level of policing in our country, Nigeria? If they are not sufficiently trained and equipped to carry out their functions, how then do we expect them to solve complicated cases? Who is the policeman that would go undercover today to solve a case? How many cases of corruption have the police, EFCC, or ICPC successfully prosecuted? How many people have our courts and judges put away for corruption? We live as if we make our own laws as we journey through life. We still see laws as those produced by the colonial masters to punish us. Hence, we must beg and bribe our ways through the law courts, when we cannot bully our way through.

Nigeria is a country of laws. We have the ability to make good and well-researched laws; a bit borrowed from the British, a bit from the USA, especially its constitution. A good number of our laws came from the military, who structured them in such a way to ensure their indefinite participation in the affairs of the nation. In the main, all laws have been made to protect the citizenry, big or small, young or old, poor or rich. If that is the case, one may ask; how come are we perceived as one of the most lawless nations of the world and fantastically corrupt?

I have travelled and lived in most parts of Nigeria, and I have observed that those that make the laws, those that wrote the constitution and made the decrees, and those whose duty it is to enforce the laws are the same people that mostly and wantonly flout the laws. The consequences of this include the fact that Nigerians respect the lawmakers but not the laws; they fear the law enforcement agencies but pay very little regard to the laws they are trying to enforce. Naturally, Nigerians are easy to govern, but lawless because of the impunity of the law breakers in high places. If we were really law-abiding, and the enforcers could do their jobs with integrity, and the leaders could exhibit a modicum of good governance, there would be very little talk about restructuring, sovereign national conference, or State policing. Rather, we would engage ourselves in such discourse as in our ability, sincerity of purpose and transparency in modifying or changing time-obsolete laws with the dictates of a dynamic society. We should advocate progressive changes with a good heart and not remain mired in archaic and feudal laws that even the most pious of nations now consider abhorrent and retrogressive. We should cease politicizing our intents and dump the notion of North or South dichotomy when we embark on any project that is for the common good. Let it be known that the killers in our judicial process are nepotism, sectional bias, cronyism, and lies.

If we must continue to see Nigeria as one, we must rise above having an Ibo leader for the Ibos, a Yoruba leader for the Yorubas, and a Northern leader for the Hausas and Fulanis. How and when can a good leader emerge so that we can face the severe security problems facing us, tackle our underperforming economy, revamp our educational sector, which is the driver of the human resource for our development as a nation? Who will lead us to understand that there can be no industrial development without a solid agricultural base and a fully developed electric power infrastructure? Who will be the leader that would encourage research into sustainable living, or that which can put us in space? Who is the leader that would actually interview a prospective minister for the portfolio that will be designated to him or her? You may ponder the relevance of all these questions to the topic, but these questions must produce the right answers from us and our leaders if we must not remain as a failed State. We cannot do the right things sought by the answers to these questions if corruption is left to thrive. And thrive, it will if the police continue to look the other way or participate in it. One last question; has anyone looked at the real costs in monetary terms, of the effect of corruption in Nigeria? I may make bold to say the cost is in excess of 250% of our GDP.

As a young man growing up, I listened to talks about the roles the Nigerian law enforcement agencies played in the various peacekeeping deployments around the world in the middle to late 20th Century. We were told that if the performances of the countries of the world were to be scored or ranked, Nigeria's scorecard would be amongst the best ten in the world. Just a few years ago, there was a gathering of police officers from many countries for some special police training programme in Houston, Texas USA. A Nigerian police officer was the best all-round student and was given a citation at the graduation ceremony. He was hosted by Nigerians in Houston, and I was present at the event, having changed my travel plans on the news of his achievements; I was proud to associate with him and to witness his moment of glory. For me, it was doubly a proud day because the officer was a DPO that was then serving in my hometown.

Today, with all due respect, our police force is a pitiable sight. A good number of them are left on the various highways where they beg for money with their guns in tow, harassing and intimidating hapless motorists. Their police stations and barracks are places you do not want to be seen going into or exiting. Some of them claim that the upkeep of their stations are sometimes funded in part by the illegal tolls they collect on the highways, and the bail monies they collect from victims of their frequent and sometimes, frivolous arrests in the communities they were meant to protect in the first place. Some also claim that they are supposed to replace their uniforms from their meagre resources, which explains why some of them who are not corruptly resourceful appear in tattered uniforms.

How did the police get to this stage? In the second half of the 80s, DSP Alozie Ogugbuaja, in an extraordinary treatise decrying the poor funding of the police institutions informed a coup-weary nation that it was in the over-arching interest of the Nigerian Army to keep the police down as an ineffective force. Ordinarily, a well-trained and well-funded police force should be able to detect a coup in the making, prevent a coup, or investigate a coup. Whether by commission or omission, this poor funding of the police has continued to this day. Worse is the practice of embezzlement and fraud within the highest echelon of the institution, exacerbating an already precarious and dangerous position the police are in. The consequence is that the police is now ill-equipped to execute its primary mandate in any manner or form. Our police cannot even mount the simplest of sting operations or infiltrate a gang in pursuit of law enforcement, or for the purpose of breaking them up. Presently, it has been reported that over half of the police force is now engaged in personal and private security details for politicians, public servants, and the rich. Under such circumstances, it is little wonder that gangs and militias can form, fester, and grow into major terrorist organisations like Boko Haram, separatist movements like MASSOB, tribal militias like OPC, Arewa Youths, MEND, etc.

In the first quarter of 2019, a campaign started on social media raising awareness to the unlawful, brutal, and torturous behaviour inflicted on young citizens of this nation, by the very organization set up to protect them. The #ENDSARS campaign raised a lot of concerns and a lot of young, affected citizens gladly shared their stories in hopes that the Federal Government can help bring the actions of SARS (Special Anti-Robbery Squad) to a complete stop or at least controlled. There were stories of SARS operatives harassing young men for flimsy reasons, without going through the proper protocol and without substantial evidence against these young men, who they arrested, bound, and took to SARS headquarters or nearby ATMs for extortion. SARS was set up as an elite team to fight the criminal cases that were beyond the police force. Why is it then that the same SARS operatives assigned to protect the citizens are the ones terrorizing them? Rather than look into the matter, the Inspector General of Police made a public announcement praising the effort of the SARS operatives and insisted that they were needed to continue the fight against armed robbery within the nation. I was disappointed by this outcome. There was photographic evidence of obvious harassment of innocent citizens being spread online, and for the IGP to publicly support these actions, it means the entire police force indeed is not fighting for the people.

As with every Nigerian civil campaign started online, the #ENDSARS flames fizzled out faster than it had started. I believe part of this was because the Police force actively tried to put an end to any offline protest going on within the nation. The protesters soon realised that life is more important than protesting a cause that was likely not going to be fulfilled.

Furthermore, the security challenges facing this nation are made worse by the porous borders and inadequate security that exist with our neighbours. Migrants from such countries like Cameroun, Niger, Chad, and the Republic of Benin, pour into Nigeria in their millions and do not return to their countries. This phenomenon bloats our population so much so that we cannot keep up with the census, but rather give estimates that are frequently being revised. This is bad for socio-economic planning. It is bad politics, and it breeds courtship with danger. A case in point is the migration of hostile Fulani herdsmen, some of whom are unauthorised aliens in the country. The actions of these marauders can pitch this nation into another civil war. These are civilians with arms carried in the open, and our police look the other way. Incredible! This cannot happen in other ECOWAS countries. Any Nigerian caught in those countries without any valid immigration papers will be dumped in jail before he can say his name.

The sad irony is that most of these countries do not harbour Nigerians the way we accept their nationals. Here in the country, they can obtain a Nigerian Passport with ease, but Nigerians who want to stay in those countries remain as aliens, if they are allowed to stay at all. These lax border controls put heavy pressure on our economic and social services, with the concomitant heating up of the polity. As I have said previously, more than a third of Nigerians have no fixed address. It is quite easy to get all these aliens out, before they take over our country. Thirty-three percent of our population is close to 66 million. We cannot afford to be silent.

Our current president came into office with the top priority of ridding the nation of corruption. However, one cannot fight corruption without sanitizing and overhauling the police institution and the judiciary. The crusade against corruption cannot begin and end in the office of the president. It ought to be anchored on the platform of our legal institutions, the rule of law, and accountability of all persons in authority, regardless of their functions. For this to be so, the police must be taught that the law is no respecter of persons, and thus, should act it out. There, lies the challenge for our leaders. If they do not imbibe these norms, eschew nepotism, they labour in vain.

Leadership In Nigeria: The Search Continues

The scene on the state of leadership in Nigeria, played itself at least half a dozen times on my mind, punctuated with innumerable, incredulous *can-you-believe-it,* as I contemplated the lecture I had been invited to deliver in Paris on leadership at the University of Schiller, as part of the graduation ceremony of the University. I was especially saddened by how hard it is to find home-grown examples of good leadership. This is an issue of grave importance to me, as in my 80+ years, I have seen my country, Nigeria, flourish under good leadership, but also see it turn to near ruins as a result of poor leadership. However, in putting together my lecture note, I decided against being like some of our leaders who speak the loudest abroad about matters affecting our domestic audience. My people have a saying, *"a good dance must commence from home."* Therefore, I will discuss part of my lecture as it relates to the Nigerian leadership situation.

Firstly, how do we define the concept of leadership? A simple definition of leadership by the Merriam-Webster dictionary is *"the power or ability to lead other people."* Ability to lead can further be distinguished by physical ability, mental ability, and in some cases, spiritual ability. The bottom line is that before an individual can assume the position of a leader, they need to have the capacity to lead. Another important characteristic of a leader is integrity. Leadership is honesty that can be held accountable to the people that are being led at any time. It is also knowing when to quit the stage; an attribute greatly lacking with most of our African leaders. At this point, I should be clear that the burden of good leadership doesn't just fall on those aiming to be leaders, but also on the led. The truth is we can't all be leaders, but we can all demand accountability in leadership like it was done in the early days of Nigeria.

Today, only the likes of Olusegun Obasanjo, T.Y Danjuma, Ibrahim Babangida, and Wole Soyinka seem to be the only ones voicing an opinion that will challenge the government. Although some of these voices might also need to answer questions.

I hope that many young people will begin to ask about what went wrong with our nation. These men are all in their late 80s, and though they are still active, there will come a day when they won't be anymore. Who will speak for the Nigerian people when they are no longer here? Who will provide insights into what Nigeria once was and can still be?

If we take time to reflect on the journey of leadership in Nigeria, from independence till date, it forces us to ask if our leaders were really prepared for the challenges and obstacles they faced on their journey. With that being said, I find it very odd that we still dip into the same pool of leaders to select our heads of government during elections. Albert Einstein would call that insanity, as he is credited with saying, *"The definition of insanity is doing the same thing over and over again but expecting different results."* In this case, we vote for the same leaders and expect change.

In a country such as Nigeria where we need strong policies put in place by young brilliant minds with vision, it is tiring to see us continue to leave the fate of this country in the hands of the geriatric population. It makes me wonder when the youth will rise and take what belongs to them. How can we say our children are the leaders of tomorrow, but we have refused to empower them to take positions of leadership? By this, I don't mean just vacating positions for them to occupy when they have not been groomed by right example to lead any differently from their predecessors. The true test of a leader's success is in his or her successor. Still, we can all agree that a man at 75 years old has no business governing a nation; instead, he should be retired, spending time with his family and serving as a mentor to the young people in leadership positions.

There was once a time in this country when a 32-year old man in the person of General Yakubu Gowon became Head of State. President Muhammadu Buhari was 41 years old when he became the military Head of State in 1983. It is quite baffling that the same man contested for and won a presidential election 30 years after his first tenure ended. I am not here to point fingers at the youth or call them names, but I think it is imperative that they take their future into their own hands for the sake of our beloved country. Leadership doesn't start at the age of 50; neither does it start at your workplace. Leadership begins in our homes, our schools, and our communities.

Back in my day, the youthful population was actively involved in the matters of our country. We took part in student body elections at the universities, and it was from there that the true leaders of our generation started to distinguish themselves, not by violence, but by strategic planning and execution. Today, I don't see that happening in our universities anymore, instead we see more of violence than strategic planning. Our youth have been distracted by all kinds of things that don't align with the vision of a better Nigeria.

There seems to be a lack of courage amongst our youth that has anchored them from reaching their full potential; they are not adequately engaged within political circles, and hence, appear to have decided, with reckless abandon, not to concern themselves with matters of the state, which unfortunately is a recipe for disaster. The leaders of today started very young and had a clear vision of what type of leaders they were going to become and when they were going to become those leaders. Has the Nigerian state completely failed the youth? I look around, and I do not see prospective young leaders anywhere. Where are this generation's Wole Soyinka, Chinua Achebe, Yakubu Gowon, Anthony Enahoro? Those who can see the void in our leadership ecosystem must endeavour to rise to help nurture these young minds so they can begin to see themselves as the leaders of tomorrow that they truly are; otherwise, it is difficult to even hope for a great future for Nigeria.

The issue of misrule and poor leadership is not exclusive to Nigeria, as many other African and non-African countries have had their fair share of the problem in varying degrees. However, unlike "the giant of Africa," Nigeria, a number of these countries have managed to and are working earnestly towards building a nation to be proud of. But Nigeria seems to be a case of growing backwards, as I am forced to wonder how we got to this point where Harvard, a world renowned university, finds it "highly educational" to study why Nigeria as a country has failed to thrive from 1960 to 1999, in respect to relative China and India, despite its endowment in human and natural resources. It had been perceived in the 70s and 80s that if there was going to be another emerging nation similar to the United States of America, it would be Nigeria because of our vast deposits of human and natural resources, but sadly in 2020, that is still not the case.

Eight Years for the South, Eight Years For the North and Zero Years For Nigeria

It is not a written law in the constitution, but to be a Nigerian is to be fully aware of the unwritten law of power-sharing in the country. This was borne out of a desire to maintain balance in the way regions get access to power. The power-sharing culture says that once a region has completed a presidency tenure (irrespective of competency), the next region on the list now has a claim to the throne. Forget the different names of candidates from varying regions; the powers that be usually would have decided the most likely candidates based on their regions.

This unwritten constitution is partly or wholly responsible for the underdevelopment of the Nigerian nation that has remained a Third World country, whereby we eat the cake and share the cake at the same time, and this is what we have done after five decades. The Nigeria that I was born into over eighty years ago, planned and executed short, medium and long-term development projects which were inherited by our founding fathers over 50 years ago. We have very little to show, and it appears that the future is going to be worse. That is so because of the sharing mentality that has eaten into our political blood cells. Even the states have started sharing development and political appointment among senatorial districts. The civil service and the local government structures have not been left out; even the traditional institutions, to the point of inventing and manufacturing traditional heads in every town and village. In the process, it has come to everyone to himself or herself, and the country, as a nation, left unattended.

This same sharing formula has distorted every developmental plan that was handed down to our founding fathers. I had mentioned earlier about the need for Nigerians to imbibe patriotism as a vital component in the pursuit of development. The love of our nation by every Nigerian, irrespective of tribe, and the respect for the national anthem and flag must be paramount, regardless of the share of the national cake.

In my research and travels around the country, I discovered that anytime an ethnic group or a local government or a political structure, even the civil service, is left out in the sharing of that national cake, the patriotism and love for the nation from that particular group vanishes into thin air, and all we hear then is marginalization. For we, the people to be able to evaluate our problems properly without referring to what the colonial masters did to us, we must get away from the blame game because the British handed over power to a solid nation that was meant to build on what was left. Nigeria had men and women of sound minds, the best you can find anywhere in the world, immense resources, and a political structure that was well-tested and still in practice in the UK and many other countries. Therefore, I cannot go on to talk about our failures without disagreeing with myself over the blame game narrative, but I must talk about the constitution prepared by us and suspended several times by us. The same military Head of State that became President through a political and democratic structure assembled the best brains in Nigeria to come up with a structure to give Nigerians a constitution that was to be the best but derailed because of a third term agenda. Then another democratically elected President followed up with yet another constitutional conference that never saw the light of the day because of the sharing mentality.

The same intrigue, as we have seen over the years, affected the development of the new city of Abuja, which was to be a milestone development and a world class city to behold. If Abuja continues with the present level of "development" the city will become a big slum in the next twenty years. The architect of the city of Abuja engaged the services of one of the best consultants in the world to develop what was to become the best new capital city to follow the movement that was made from Rio to Brasilia in Brazil and from Sidney to Cambria in Australia. These countries made their moves just before us and were visited by our consultants mainly to learn from their mistakes because you don't make such a monumental move without running into crises. But from what I have seen over the development in the last twenty years, mistakes upon mistakes have been made because at a stage the masterplan was abandoned.

I was one of the first people that worked in the new capital city when it was no city. I had to operate from Suleja, about an hour drive to the city of Abuja because there was not even a place to stay in Abuja. Few years into the building of the new capital city, the sharing of positions, sharing of lands, and sharing of the cake made nonsense of what was intended, and the masterplan was no longer adhered to. I was part of a team that established a soil database for the whole territory, thereby any building of a major infrastructure must refer to the database before designing the foundation of such a structure.

For me then, the building of a new city from scratch was to showcase the immense human resources that were put together, drawing Nigerians from every part of the world, from ministries and professional bodies. Not too long ago, I was shocked to know that the authorities did not know about the soil database. In all my activism, as some may see me, especially since turning eighty, I not only stated the problems as I saw them, backed by facts, I also proffered solutions to the issues that have befallen our nation.

Therefore, we the people must admit that we have failed our nation in many ways. We must not wait to be told by outsiders anymore. We must learn from what was done with the telecommunication industry that made it possible for the poor to own phones. The same partnership can be introduced so that the poor can have electricity and water. The same partnership can be employed to give our nation airways, airports, trains, and railways. The same can be done with our steel plants, refineries, the automobile assembly plants, paper mills, the river basin authorities, and saving Lake Chad for our agricultural pursuit. We borrowed money from around the world to prepare the nation for industrial take-off many decades ago, but somewhere down the road, we have presided over the collapse of that foundation. And we spend almost half of our resources servicing our debts despite the debt forgiveness that was offered by both London and the Paris Club.

My take, therefore, is that if Nigeria must move away from the present quagmire, we must step back a little, accept our failures and begin a process of repositioning so that we the people can make and rebuild once again. For the sake of the present and future generation, we, the present actors, must leave the nation a better place than we met it, and we must start to change today, not tomorrow.

Nigeria In Trouble Once Again

As I remember the 41st United States President, George H. W. Bush, who passed November 2018, I couldn't help but admire and respect him immensely. He served only one term but became best of friends till death with the President who defeated and denied him a second term. This is a lesson for our politicians and students of politics; for among observers of the Nigerian democratic elections, there is often an unspoken but well-known axiom to the effect that there hardly has been a smooth and peaceful election where the sitting president relinquish power willingly to the winning candidate without malicious opposition and questionable acts to discredit the candidate and undermine the votes.

As the next election looms, I see a nation in trouble once again. Most politicians have come to agree that our political structure is not working; a good number say that the economy is fragile and fading, even as Nigerians have accepted that the safety and security of the populace is not guaranteed, and that has affected the mental state of the people, particularly those that live in the IDP camp. During the last few years, the standard of education being offered to the present generation, who will become leaders of tomorrow, is flawed and has no learning potential; thus, the future is bleak, and we, the people must stand up and be counted.

Every time I reflect on matters affecting Nigeria, I am constantly thinking about the generation that will inherit the future. The generation that will be gifted the future had no role in the outcome but will need to work through blood and sweat to brighten it. I can only say that the present generation and past, especially those of us between 65 and 85 years must be held responsible. My generation took so much from Nigeria and gave back so little. Now, we are departing the earth, leaving it in a worse state than we met it.

Right before our eyes, despite the privilege of having the best of two worlds, the foundation of our nation, though largely influenced by the British, was crashed, and the immense resources that followed the independence were mismanaged or outrightly stolen. We began to thrive at tearing the country apart and dividing it to a point of no return so that all that is left is the transition from one crisis to another, which only serves to hold back the emergence of the nation's once great potential.

Asking questions and holding elders responsible for the trouble we are in today is against the culture of many Nigerian tribes, but I have always opposed this and made it a point to tell my children and grandchildren, both biological and non-biological, to start now to ask questions before it is too late. My generation must be asked, "how come that the many nations of the world where Nigerians work in every capacity are building centres in Space and all we have done is build castles in the air?" More questions like, "how come my generation got good education and learning yet all we could offer the next generation after us was some education but no learning?" I recall that with only five or six universities in the country, the standards and infrastructure were of world standards; students came from across Africa and the world to study in Nigeria. Today, Nigerians are travelling anywhere and everywhere to find quality education.

During the 2019 election campaigns, I listened to several interviews and debates from almost all the aspirants, and it left me with "if only." I have travelled far and wide, and I have never known any country that possesses a combination of the class, the intelligence, and the leadership credentials that the young men and women of our country exhibited. This intelligence and leadership credentials were seen from the well-articulated programme they have for the office to the well-prepared manifestos being dished out to the people, as well as the love they proclaim to have for their nation.

There was still the norm, though: we saw candidates unable to articulate their plans or completely disregarding the need to since they hold power at the moment and or have the money to 'buy' the votes. And of course, there was also the usual theatrics that comes up during elections amongst the different parties.

However, I have a question for those who want to give the country a change or a different direction: "Where have you all wonderful politicians or magicians been all these years?" I listened to some of them and they made the Clinton and Obama debate of 2010 look so ordinary. Even Putin of Russia debating the press in his one-party structure did not possess the convincing posture that was displayed by our presidential aspirants. I found myself pondering on this so much that I could not help but ask that question. Is this a case of "the beautiful ones have now been born" or Nigerians have simply had enough? Maybe it is both. Then, my "if only" led me to the more important question: "Would there ever be a chance of victory for any of these wonderful candidates in a system so steeped in corruption? "

For the latter, my ever-hopeful self believes so. However, there would need to be much sacrifices and unity, as there can only be, after all, one captain on a ship. From the eight to ten young presidential aspirants that I listened to, most of them can give the nation the leadership it desires, but there can only be one president at a time. Therefore, they must all get together and start to prepare for a journey that will take not less than eight years to dismantle the present political structure that has held this country in bondage for decades. Sadly, it won't happen now, but the bricks of the wall of fake democracy can begin to fall from now. During that journey, a true leader will emerge amongst them that will take this country to the Promised Land. It is only by agreeing amongst themselves to appoint a leader that the process of restructuring, reshaping, and repositioning of the country can commence for the sake of the coming generation.

Idle Minds: Woes of An Unproductive Population

At dawn on this particular Tuesday, a major story made the headlines in the media. It was the statement by a man who I dearly respect; Nigeria's former Army Chief and Minister of Defence, Lt Gen Theophilus Danjuma (Retired), on the need for Nigerians to defend themselves against the ongoing widespread massacres across the nation.

For some, his statement was a reckless call for anarchy at a time when already there have been talks of war, impending or imagined. For others, it resonates with reality. A reality filled with the pain and languishes of many Nigerians who have lost friends, families, and property to the onslaught of attacks by terrorists masquerading as cattle breeders. A reality that clearly shows that our government has failed us; the security agencies have failed to protect us.

However, I will like to once again caution members of both camps; let us not talk about war, because if it happens, there will be nothing left of Nigeria. If war occurs, there will be no flow of oil; there will be no safe grazing fields for the cattle; the farmers will have no produce, leading to food scarcity and starvation. Indeed, the country may disintegrate into anarchy, which is worse than war because with anarchy you will not know who your enemy is or where to find him, as over a third of our population has no address.

As frightening as the situation is now, it may only get worse. Nigeria is blessed with ample natural resources that can last decades, vast green lands suitable for agriculture, rivers and lakes for fishing activities and more importantly, we are blessed with human resources that rivals no other country in the continent of Africa. Nigeria recorded a population of 185 million people in 2016 and with a 2.5% yearly growth, that number is said to rise much more by 2020. Looking at these numbers, it can be said that we have a sizable population that can drive economic growth in any industry. Unfortunately, this hasn't been the case. A large portion of its enviable population size is filled with unemployed and unemployable people. The illiteracy rate in this country is staggering. With an illiterate population of 65 million to 70 million people, one can argue that this is cause for alarm. All these negative factors have arisen because of our government's lack of farsightedness and their inability to adjudge the impact of our unproductive population growth and its demand-generated problems in the economy.

Another fact is that Nigeria, Africa's most populous country, is witnessing a growing youth bulge, with those under 14 years accounting for more than 40 percent of its citizens, according to the National Population Commission. To be exact, we are a country with one of the largest populations of youth in the world. This unlimited unproductive population bulge constitutes the primary reason for most of the ills Nigeria is facing, economically, socially, and environmentally. If half of the population isn't actively engaged in any enterprise, what else do you think will occupy their attention? The famous saying that an idle man is the devil's workshop rings very true here. From the herdsmen to the militias in the Niger Delta and the terrorists in the north, a common factor is the heavy presence of youth. Hence, this title: *Idle Minds – Woes of An Unproductive Population.*

Education is a vital part of civilization. A glaring feature of an underdeveloped economy is the poor quality of the human capital as a result of poor educational standards, which is the main factor behind the all-round backwardness of our polity. Illiteracy not only retards people's growth but also keeps people's outlook and thought-process in a constant negative downward direction. Any society that is passionate about its development must educate its people; no nation can be greater than its level of education. What happened to our Education sector? What happened to our Universities? Nigeria used to boast of prestigious higher Institutions that graduated the finest of scholars. Somewhere along the line, we lost our foresight, and we have ourselves to blame for that. It's no wonder that even the Minister of Education and distinguished members of our ailing government will rather send their children to universities abroad.

There has been a steady migration of Nigeria scholars to Universities all around the world. Every year, our children flood the halls of institutions in these foreign lands. Some of them never return home as they find that the grass might indeed be much greener on the other side. Meanwhile, their counterparts in our once prestigious universities have to fight semester after semester for something close to decent university education. When the universities are not on strike, the classrooms are overpopulated, making it a herculean task to learn or get a proper education. Along the line, due to the frustration of an unsatisfactory university experience, they turn to activities that don't necessarily set them on the course for a brighter future. Sadly, our government has failed our children.

Our top priority in this country should be investing in our people. We need to take advantage of the human resources we have been blessed with. Policies should be put in place, and plans should be made to ensure that education in this country is not an afterthought. It should be at the forefront of any economic recovery plan prepared by the government.

I have had the opportunity of travelling to different parts of Nigeria, and one thing that still shocks me till date is the extreme level of illiteracy and poverty that has ravaged Northern Nigeria. Yobe State, for example, has a literacy level of about seven percent, which is currently the lowest in the country. This is followed closely by Zamfara state, with a recorded literacy level of about 19 percent. Taraba State, on the other hand, has a literacy level of 72 perecnt, but that is still miles behind a state like Lagos State with a recorded literacy level of about 95 percent.

In recent times, much insurgency has stemmed from Northern Nigeria. We have been unfortunate enough to witness terrorist groups like Boko Haram, whose major activities are carried out in Northern Nigeria. If we take our time to analyse this situation, a direct link can be traced back to illiteracy. When a group of able-bodied men have nothing to do, the devil will surely take advantage of their idleness to propagate his malicious agenda.

Here's a scenario: During one of FADE's numerous tree planting activities, we voyaged to Makoda local government in Kano State for the Makoda Wall of Trees project. Because of the amount of time we spent there, I became quite popular among the locals and every time I go back to visit, an entourage of no less than 100 men awaited my arrival. It was always a bittersweet feeling seeing a lot of young men in their 20s, 30s and 40s waiting around for me on a working day. They will then follow me to my final place of residence and sometimes camp outside for days because they know I usually gift them a small stipend to be shared amongst them. Each ended up with a tiny amount of money, which is not justified by the amount of time they had spent with me.

The problem here is not even unemployment; this can easily be solved by creating jobs. However, it's a different case here where you have middle-aged men who are unemployable, which means even if there are jobs, these men will be unable to do the jobs. How did we get to this point? We let illiteracy spread too far into our communities, and now we have a big problem on our hands. A big problem that has left our youth malleable to manipulation by the highest bidder seeking to wreak havoc in the nation.

If we journey down to Southern Nigeria, we find a similar problem there. Men whose lands have been devastated by aggressive oil exploration activities are scattered all over the place. These men no longer have farmlands to grow their crops; their rivers and lakes are home to oil spills that render it useless to any fishing activities. When we have a group of desperate men who feel like so much has been taken from them without any form of compensation, we begin to see insurgency rise in the form of militants and terrorists. This is where we find ourselves today as a country. We are a country that only just decades ago had functional industries that could provide well over 10 million direct jobs across the federation and more when enhanced.

The only way for us to come out of this quagmire is to revive our failed industries. We need to admit to ourselves that it is not an absolute lack of funds that has caused our infrastructural decay but outright mismanagement of these funds. We are not cursed but corrupt, or maybe we are both cursed and corrupt. So, the questions then become: How do we engage our youth? How do we prioritize their future? We owe it to them to create an environment where they can thrive because if we don't, we are sitting on a ticking time bomb that will explode soon.

Beyond Buhari and Atiku

The political and ruling class that has emerged over the last five decades and more may have rescued the nation from many struggles and catastrophes such as the struggle for independence, the political rascality that followed the independence: the coups and the civil war. They may even have also rescued the country from religious apathy, worse financial mismanagement leading to bankruptcy and many more disasters that would have befallen the nation far before now. For such great service, I often feel that the ruling class particularly those from my generation must believe that Nigerians and Nigeria must still be largely indebted to them, even though some of them went away with choice national honours. How else can we explain their refusal to give up power and retire from the battleground that is Nigeria's political scene?

To ensure the sustainability of their staying power, these 'warriors or heroes' of the country have developed a system of godfatherism. On the one hand, to fund and endorse their campaigns, while on the other hand, they have employed agents of no-change, whose key role is to maintain the status quo until such a time as when the chosen 'heir apparent' takes over from them. This keeps power in the family.

It appears that until we find out what exactly we owe and pay up our debts, these 'creditors', these powers-that-be will continue to hold back the country in bondage for the next 50 years, and the development of the nation which we have continued to promise our children, grandchildren, and the next generation of leaders will never happen. I recall that my generation and the generation before me used to sing a song about youth with the first line that goes thus, *"We are the leaders of tomorrow ..."* However, sadly enough, over 50 years down the line, we have not only become leaders of tomorrow, but we are also now even the future leaders. The same leaders of those days remain the leaders of today. The same leaders that have continued to truncate and slow down the emergence of the nation despite the human and natural resources that abound in the country. I have come to discover that this generation of leaders continually slows down the nation's growth by investing heavily in unproductive sectors while neglecting more productive sectors, such that instead of regenerating the country, these leaders end up regenerating themselves.

In one of my writings, I discussed the difference between a fractured nation, which I believe is Nigeria's diagnosis, and a severe head injury, which J.K Randle believed was affecting Nigeria. According to J.K Randle, what the nation has been experiencing is a severe head injury, but in my article, "A Fractured Nation," I argued that a severe head injury could lead to a coma and possibly death which would be the end of the nation, but a fracture can be repaired or renewed if necessary attention is paid to it. I still believe the latter is true, and Nigeria isn't beyond redemption.

In my 80+ years in this wonderful nation, Nigeria, I have been fortunate to have travelled and lived in almost every part of Nigeria. I have also visited and lived in almost all civilized nations of the globe. I have explored mountains, some deserts of the world, seas and oceans, and having seen how beautiful our planet earth was, is and can be, my dream then and now is that I must make this planet a better place than I met it. The generation before mine did the same and made it possible for me to experience this wonderful world. Thus, my writings come from a place of hope and frustration because I have lived in a world that worked and a nation that fitted well in that working world. This is what drives me to prepare a succession team of warriors and writers, who have sometimes travelled with me and shared with me the deplorable disintegration and insecurity into which the country is gradually slipping.

With time, this team of successors will join and continue the activism because we must continue to share and create awareness through our numerous audiences on the need for the younger generation to prepare themselves for the work ahead. In history, we were told that the French revolution started after the many failures of leadership in France. The Nigerian situation as it stands today has recorded many failures; some of them have been mentioned and discussed in my writings. With our many failures, it is time for a revolution, and sadly, that revolution cannot be led by the same people who have been a part of the rot. Hence, this title, "Beyond Buhari and Atiku". I have met both men, and have the utmost respect for them, but since the return to democratic rule in 1999, our elections have been a case of the devil and the deep blue sea.

Therefore, considering that we have been misruled

for the last 50 years, my question is, "Can we have anything different from the same party, albeit different names, especially when they have been a part of this misrule?" At the same time, if we are to have a new generation of leaders after eight years; is there enough time for them to emerge? This is because, contrary to the current style for prospective leaders, emerging leadership happens way before becoming presidential aspirants. Prospective leaders need to travel around the country to be seen and heard. Serve in numerous capacities that will build their portfolios of a proven track record both in public and private sectors.

Summarily, beyond Muhammadu Buhari and Atiku Abubakar lies our nation's future; a future we need to seriously prepare for so that it won't be a replica of the past. Millions of Nigerians are fed up with the status quo that only benefits the same select few over and over. Budding leaders will have much to deal with, but sadly, I fear the next election might not be when they start to clear this rot. What these budding leaders need right now are mobilizers who will sensitize the people as well as ignite their passion for a revolution. These budding leaders also need funders that won't demand kickbacks like the "godfathers." Funders from the people who would eagerly contribute towards a better nation like was done in America for Bernie Sanders. If these vibrant young people, tired of the rot in the nation, can come together, mobilize themselves and begin to sensitize the people towards thinking of a future without the present leaders, albeit a process that may still take some years, then Nigeria stands a chance of escaping the cycle of corruption and mismanagement that has plagued her for decades.

Dividends of Democracy

Democracy defined in its simplest form means, the government of the people, for the people, and by the people. This definition simply means that the people, the citizens are the major stakeholders in decision making, and all issues of national importance are decided in accordance with their wishes and aspirations. What happens is that the people vote and send their representatives to take up the office, where they are genuinely represented without any bias or personal considerations. These representatives are supposed to be selfless and true custodians of national interests; owing allegiance only to the country, not to themselves or their respective parties and financial supporters; thus, they must consider themselves bound to contribute in the best interest of the country.

When we embraced democracy in Nigeria, this is

the fantastic deal we signed up for, but sadly, we have continually received the opposite. Therefore, I hope to pass across a message that will encourage my fellow Nigerians to ponder over the state of our democracy, and I hope you will agree with me when I say we need to evaluate the democratic agreement we have made with our political leaders.

Some time ago, a governor made a speech assuring the people of his State that his administration would continue in its efforts to develop the State and deliver "the dividends of democracy to all." This phrase got me thinking about what was implied as against what often happens. Many of us have come across the word 'dividend' on many occasions. The word, as used in business terms, is defined as "payment made by a corporation to its shareholders to distribute the profit." As noted above, democracy is a government elected by the people and obligated to govern with the interest of the masses at heart. Therefore, the dividends of democracy are simply the benefits enjoyed by the masses who voted for the government in power.

If we draw parallels between Nigeria and a company listed on the Nigerian Stock Exchange, we will be able to see how terrible the pay-out on our investments in the country is. The last thing a smart businessperson will do is invest money in a business that rarely pays dividends, has a terrible balance sheet, records capital losses year after year and finally, shows no room or definite plans for growth. When a company like this exists, the board of directors will usually come together to discuss a way forward so that the shareholders can benefit from their investments, or the shareholders will move to replace the members of the board who have proven incompetent at running a successful company.

If an entrepreneur is a person who habitually creates and innovates to build something of recognized value around perceived opportunities; how will we define a political entrepreneur? He or she must be one who understands and uses the opportunity to create and innovate something of value for himself or herself with capital raised by the masses.

Every election year we go to vote in new officials, we must remember that we are investing in a government that will either return a favourable dividend to us or not. We shouldn't settle for the little gifts and pay-outs during the campaigns because, as shareholders of this country, we deserve to reap the full benefits of our democracy. In their usual fashion, politicians would be seen making grand gestures in the communities six months before the elections. Why do they do this? Is it because they have tunnel vision and can only see what benefits them, or is it because they believe the little gifts and handouts are the dividends of democracy the masses should expect from them?

The inequality in the country is at an all-time high. Our middle class is evaporating, and many people are one major illness or financial burden away from poverty. Alas, the dividends of democracy are not equally shared. You will be forgiven if you, like me, had once thought to describe the "dividends of democracy" as the presence of good roads, potable water supply, accessible and affordable education, affordable quality healthcare, constant power supply, high employment rates, good transport system, affordable housing, and favourable economy for trade and investment, just to mention a few. Forgiven for being highly mistaken. As for the politicians, power is the greatest dividend, and numerous other benefits accompany that power. Foreign trips, flashy cars, extravagant lifestyles, are just some of the benefits waiting for a politician and those who have invested in them when they win the election. The majority shareholders with their 'perceived measly votes' are left with bad roads, weak infrastructure, poor electricity, lousy governance, etc.

That is why it baffles me that some people still don't vote. You matter more than you think in the landscape of Nigerian democracy. Every great successful revolution was won primarily by perseverance. It is unwise to sit back and lament that one's vote doesn't count in the hope that someday that will change miraculously without having to raise a finger. Your greatest weapon as a citizen is your vote, and that should be wielded with valour and strength. We are a nation of hardworking, ambitious people that can often be found almost anywhere in the world involved in one business or the other and doing well. Nigerians are known as, in colloquial lingua, 'hustlers', yet in the one thing that is probably the most important, most of us choose to be unlike what we are known for.

In the last election, only about 67,000,000 people were registered to vote. Out of this number, only 43.65% came out to vote. The number of people who voted was not up to 20% of our entire population. If we keep sitting out the election process, it will be difficult for us to witness the change that we seek. I believe it is easier to inflate figures than it is to deflate them, so let's stop making things easy for those who wish to 'pad' our votes in their favour.

Dr. Kingsley Ozumba Mbadiwe coined the term "men of timber and calibre", and became famously known by that, in one of his many colourful speeches as a member of the House of Representatives, former Minister of Lands, Minister of Trade and

Commerce, and Minister of Aviation. Perhaps at that time, he meant it as a way to describe men who were steady and of strong character like the timber, though I am still trying to understand what the calibre connotes. But in all, we have come to accept it as the norm when describing politicians during campaign rallies and other ego fanning functions. Somehow, I feel Mbadiwe would be appalled at its current use.

It shouldn't be a matter of debate that a democratic government is one that exists primarily to protect, provide basic goods and services, and increase the quality of life of every member of the society it serves. It shouldn't, but as we have come to see, this is many times not the case for our "men of timber and calibre." So next time one of our dear politicians uses the phrase, "dividends of democracy," can he be so kind as to explain what he truly means, so we are not disappointed or confused when the outcome doesn't align with our expectations.

PART II

OIL AND DIVISION

"Like a pebble tossed into a pond, an oil shock creates ripples or effects felt everywhere... It is in our best interest to embark on a revolutionary change that will lead us away from oil dependency rather than drag our feet and [continue to] suffer the costs of dependency on a diminishing resource"

— Albert Marrin

The Cheap Oil Wealth

For many underdeveloped nations, finding valuable natural resources can have perverse and economically destructive consequences; as with such wealth, if not carefully managed can breed autocratic leadership, undermining democracy, and place the nation on a dangerous relationship with violent conflicts and poverty. In many underdeveloped countries, the oil has brought neither sustained economic growth nor social improvements; the wealth it creates is spent with careless abandon by a select few, disrupting normal behaviour and instigating unrealistic expectations.

In Nigeria, the oil came to us cheap and caught us completely unprepared. We didn't expect it, so we didn't prepare for it and then became wholly incapable of managing it. Soon after the oil came, we started slowing down on agriculture, manufacturing and expanding our industries. Oil became our newfound love, and we had eyes only for it, everything else faded from our line of sight.

We discovered oil in 1958, and it has since the early 1970s dominated the economy. Today, Nigeria is the largest oil producer in sub-Saharan Africa, and since 1971, a member of OPEC (Organization of the Petroleum Exporting Countries), with an estimated production volume of 2.413 million barrels per day as at 2005. This makes it the world's sixth largest producer.

The political structure that was established between the colonial government and our founding fathers was disbanded or suspended to be replaced with coups, wars, and massive corruption. We started dividing the nation because of oil and Nigeria has never been the same ever since. This once lush and green nation has become eerily divided militarily, politically and structurally. The constitution we uphold is not acceptable to many Nigerians because of the marginalization that the emergence of oil encouraged. The young intellects, thinkers, scientist, inventors, and teachers stopped thinking because everyone's success story could be found in the oil industry. The international financial institutions started lending us the money we didn't need or even know how to manage because we had the oil they wanted. And of course, as with everything cheap or stolen by many, sharing became a big problem. This became our Nigerian problem; an unacceptable sharing formula, and it appears the problem will remain with us for a very long time.

Notably, Nigeria is in the top ten list of the world's largest producers of oil, yet with its estimated population of 200 million, ranks atop the list as the nation with the world's highest number of poor people, just over 91 million higher than former reigning champion, India, whose total population of 1.3 billion more than triples Nigeria's.

Low human development level, social conflicts and environmental degradation are just a few problems which characterise the state of development in Nigeria. The mind-boggling question is why a country that is so highly endowed with one of the most valuable resources has fared so disproportionally poorly in economic and social terms.

For over forty years, we have talked about diversifying the economy so that we can rely less on oil revenue but have achieved very little progress on that. Many countries that discovered oil about the same time with Nigeria have not only taken their population out of poverty, but many have gone from

- Insurgence may also be on the rise, which will affect production and distribution.

- Most things that depend almost solely on oil money may go into esteem.

With all these in mind, I am reminded of the scripture I encountered over seventy years ago in the Bible from the book of Mathew Chapter 25 verses 14 – 30 about the parable of the bags of gold. It was told that a certain man going on a journey called his servants and entrusted them with his wealth: *"To one, he gave five bags of gold, to another two bags, and another one bag, each according to his ability. Then he went on his journey."* We are told that after a long time, the master of those servants returned and settled accounts with them.

The man who had received five bags of gold brought an additional five. *"Master,"* he said, *"you entrusted me with five bags of gold. See, I have gained five more."* The man with two bags of gold also doubled his. It was then down to the one that was given a bag. *"Master,"* he said, *"I knew that you are a hard man, harvesting where you have not sown and gathering where you have not scattered seed. So, I was afraid and went out and hid your gold in the ground. See, here is what belongs to you."* The master was upset and took the bag of gold from him and gave it to the one that now had ten.

He said in verse 29, "… *For whoever has will be given more, and they will have an abundance. Whoever does not have, even what they have will be taken from them.*"

Nigeria is like the servant with one bag of gold and its oil is the gold. Let's hope what we have and haven't used wisely won't be taken away from us and given to others more deserving.

Nigeria Without Oil

In a campaign to look beyond oil and explore other resourceful avenues of development and wealth in the State, the former Governor of Delta State, Dr. Emmanuel Eweta Uduaghan coined the phrase *"Delta without oil"* in a State that is the highest oil-producing area in the country. Although the campaign didn't result in the expected outcome, the phrase remains with me and in the process generated the title: Nigeria without oil.

In the previous piece, I shared a story about the dinner event that I was privileged to attend in honour of the Rwandan President, Paul Kagame. The host, Ambassador Dele Cole had mentioned how oil was a curse to Nigeria, and the Rwandan President who was at this time looking into the possibility of oil exploration in his country reacted to the Ambassador's speech by saying if oil is a curse, then he would like to have the curse in his country.

That is not the first time the oil has been labelled a curse. Former Venezuelan Oil Minister and OPEC co-founder, Juan Pablo Perez Alfonzo, was the first to draw attention to the problem of oil; he said, *"Oil is not black gold; it is the devil's excrement."* However, before I go into whether the oil is a curse or not to Nigeria, I'd like to touch on various ways in which the country survived without oil, especially dating back to the 40s and 50s which was the time during which I transitioned from childhood to adulthood.

During that era, most parts of Nigeria did not have electricity. Instead, we depended on lanterns at night, and gas lamps for the elites on occasions. For most parts of Nigeria, the full moon was a major source of energy and that was when the young came out to play. That was also the time most people experienced romance for the first time.

We harvested rainwater for domestic use and supplemented the other purposes with water from rivers. Bridges and Roads were built to international standards and maintained by road overseers who were on hand to patch up potholes whenever and wherever they occurred. There were Post Offices everywhere, and it took no more than three to four days for letters to travel to any part of the country. Telegrams took 24 hours to get to their destinations within the country.

There was Train service from the South to the North, and there was very little food importation. The Northern part of Nigeria exported Groundnut for their foreign exchange. The Groundnut pyramids were a sight to behold and a huge tourist attraction at the time.

The western part of Nigeria exported Cocoa. The income brought development to a good part of western Nigeria with Cocoa houses scattered around the region for everybody to see. Also, western Nigeria was the first region to build a television station in the continent of Africa. Mid-Western Nigeria had Palm oil, and the value chain generated millions of employment. Eastern Nigeria was a region dominated with trade and commerce; they also had a bit of Palm oil.

From my recollection, Nigeria did not borrow more than she earned from exports. Our Nigerian pound was stronger than the US dollar and almost at par with the British pound. Our educational standard was rivalled only by that of the British and was better than the United States. Religious institutions like Christianity and Islam were private. They built schools, colleges and hospitals all over the country as part of their evangelical mission to draw members to themselves.

Our medical institutions which employed a combination of traditional and conventional methods were reasonably adequate, and I cannot recall Nigerians travelling abroad for medicals the way we do today. Our education and health systems were such that attracted people from other African countries. This was the Nigeria that I loved to the point that I declined several opportunities to take up dual citizenship during the course of my work in the UK and the US. I was proud of our green passport. Sadly, our green passport today has become a source of embarrassment.

Today, the Nigeria with oil that I have come to know and that we are bequeathing to the generation after us is a different Nigeria. It is a Nigeria that once ran a national airline which started with 28 planes and infrastructures, not only all over Nigeria but in major cities of the world, and now cannot even boast of one aircraft. A country that began with six universities and teaching hospitals attracting students and patients from all over the continent due to the quality of education being offered, but today, we have well over a hundred universities that provide some learning but no education.

We built super-highways like the Lagos – Ibadan expressway, but that fell apart in a period of 10 years. We built six refineries yet in the last 25 years we've been importing refined petroleum products from those countries that buy our crude, while we watch the collapse of the refineries one after the other.

We also built six motor vehicle assembly plants with a view of developing secondary industries and gradually reducing the importation of the vehicles and parts. However, almost 40 years down the line, these assembly plants are still importing 100 percent TKD, whereas by now, these plants should have been generating millions of employments in the secondary industries built to support the assembly plants. There were also six steel mills, but they also met the same fate as our refineries.

All the things listed above were supposed to be the beginning of the industrialization of Nigeria; not only funded by money from oil, but this process was also supported by funds borrowed from London and Paris club. The loans were later to haunt Nigeria before the arrival of Ngozi Okonjo-Iweala, who negotiated debt relief for the country.

Looking at where we were before oil and where we are today as a country with oil money supported by borrowed funds meant to bring about the industrialization of the country, many are left wondering how it is that we still remain underdeveloped.

One would expect that by now the Nigeria my generation should be handing over to our children would be better and more developed. However, this is, sadly, not the case. This is worsened by the fact that nobody has been held accountable for the mismanagement and derailment of the many initiatives started in the 60s, 70s and 80s.

In as much as I do not want to take Nigeria back to my stone age; a time when we had no water or power, I can't help but refer to those days more fondly than I do the present. If we must engage in the transformation of the country, then we must do everything in our power to avoid the mismanagement of the past. If one is to go by the letter exchanged between President Mohammadu Buhari and former president, Olusegun Obasanjo, highlighting the problem of having power without Power, building refineries without refined products, waterworks without water, and public works department without good roads, there may be no change in sight. It is time to appeal to the leaders of this country to stop politicising all the issues at stake and focus on what will bring about a Nigeria that was the dream of our founding fathers.

There are three areas I would like to point out:

- The environment was once clean and healthy because we had sanitary inspectors.

- The council of states is a platform where former heads of states, governors, and chief security officers of the states meet to deliberate issues at stake. Recall that President Obasanjo is a member of this council. Topical issues raised in his thought-provoking open letter to Buhari would have been better discussed at this platform.

- Bearing in mind that nations of the world that have committed to the Paris Climate Change protocol have started the implementation of the protocol. This will eventually bring about a reduction in energy requirements coupled with the fact that the USA has started drilling new fields which will also reduce their energy requirements from Nigeria, Saudi Arabia and other oil-producing countries. Also worthy of note is the fact that most European countries have been carrying out research and developing electric vehicles. At the time all these innovations come on stream, the appetite for crude oil will drastically reduce, which will also crash the price of crude oil, and that could spell doom for Nigeria.

Summarily, Nigeria needs to position herself to function without crude oil and now is the time to start, not tomorrow. We are entering a new phase, as there are many doubts regarding oil as a reliable economic resource, and many countries are currently seeking more reliable alternatives to oil. To continue to function according to the old logic of sole dependence on oil may lead to the collapse of the economy soon, due to dangerous shifts in the oil alternatives market.

On the question of oil being a curse or not to Nigeria; I will say, we have to decide on what we want it to be by our actions. If the wealth of oil is used wisely, it will change the future of the nation for generations to come, making it a blessing, but if it's abused and misused, neglecting other sectors of development on its account, as is currently the case, it will impoverish the country, making it poorer than it was before discovering oil; thus, a curse.

The Threat to Nigeria's Development: The Three "R"

Over time, I have come to realise that there are three "R" at the root cause of the majority of Nigeria's problems, and I want to discuss these three "R", which I believe are threatening the development and the existence of Nigeria: Resource Control, Religion, and Restructuring.

I will be discussing these topics in a way that relates to the Nigerian narrative. I have always maintained that for us to succeed in the future, we need to go back to the past and examine where we got it wrong so that we don't repeat the same mistakes in the future. Let's start with resource control.

- ## Resource Control

We cannot talk about Resource Control without

mentioning how this particular subject was partly responsible for the civil war of 1967 to 1970, lasting for three years. Resource control put a halt to the mediation that attempted to prevent an all-out civil war. This mediation attempt is popularly known as the Aburi Accord and was held between 4th and 5th January 1967 in Aburi, Ghana.

At the time the accord was reached, the Federal Government of Nigeria realized that the agreement wouldn't favour the nation as a whole. The Aburi accord was based or structured on a loose federation giving more power to the regions. Seeing that the Federal Government would have had little control over the major resources of the nation if the accord was followed to the later, Gen. Yakubu Gowon's led military administration decided not to accommodate the accord, since it meant relinquishing autonomous control of the resources for which it had begun to develop keen interest. Instead, it was re-interpreted to suit their purposes.

Following the re-evaluation of the accord, a significant part of the entire eastern region of Nigerian, which was later known as Biafra, objected strongly to the Federal Government's interpretation of the accord.

Furthermore, Resource Control led to the origin

of what we know and describe as insurgency, particularly in the Niger Delta. Let us keep in mind that the whole of Eastern Nigeria that was to become Biafra was where most of the crude oil of the country was located and still is located. If Biafra had succeeded in occupying the then "Bendel" region the way it was intended, the entire oil resources of the country would have been under the control of a foreign land. Foreign because the secession that Biafrans were fighting for, if gotten, would have meant they would no longer be a part of Nigeria. Nigeria will then have little or no oil to call its own.

The Civil war might have ended, but the issue of Resource Control hasn't been addressed and many of the problems that followed the exploration of oil, which includes, the pollution of the rivers and water bodies, negative health implications, unemployment, crimes such as armed robbery and kidnapping, are still with us today.

Isn't it time we start looking at a nation without oil? Maybe if we do so, it will allow for a smoother restructuring process. I must commend the former Governor of Delta State, Dr. Emmanuel Eweta Uduaghan, for first coining the phrase "Delta Without Oil" in a state that is the highest producing oil state in the country. Although the campaign didn't result in the outcome many of us had hoped for, but the phrase remained with me. We need to be able to tell ourselves the hard truth and stop looking at matters with wool in our eyes or Nigeria will not survive much longer.

• Religion

Religion plays a significant role in the way we live our daily lives as Nigerians. I will use a personal tale to describe my thoughts on this topic. Many years ago, in my pursuit for equity and giving back to my community, I had constructed a borehole in my town to stop the people from fetching water from a river that was beginning to be badly polluted and acidic, and also about five kilometres away from the town. The borehole program, which was commissioned by the then Military Governor of Bendel State, Jeremiah Oseni, was part of some projects I was working on to help the town. I followed up this charitable act by giving a 28-Seater bus to a popular Catholic Convent in the same town; then fencing a school and Church premises for the Anglican community. I had planned nothing else until the Muslim community approached me sometime later to assist with the building of a mosque. After looking at what it would cost, I agreed to do this for them. This singular act of kindness almost got me in trouble with my town. Their reason being that I, a

Christian, was trying to Islamize my town. My saving grace was that the visit of the Emir of Kano, the late Alhaji Ado Bayero, who was available for the commissioning of the Mosque, brought almost half of the country to my town to witness an unprecedented carnival, and the media had reported it as a case of how people of different faiths can live together in harmony. The good publicity doused the anger of the Christian community, as they then realised that a simple "God's work" even to those not a part of your religion could benefit a small town. I was now known as a man who made Akwukwu the place where Christians and Muslims lived in peace and harmony.

My story on religion doesn't end with the Christians and the Muslims. Way before those two religions, Nigeria had its own religious practices, and I have always respected that. A traditional meeting place of my hometown known as the Ogwa Obi, built hundreds of years ago, started falling apart due to wear and tear that comes with a place that old. In the usual fashion of traditional norm, the Kingmakers began insinuating that the problems of the town (most of which could be attributed to climate change, poor healthcare facilities, bad roads, and the other culprits) were due to the absence of a proper meeting place. They claimed that the gods were angry. Secondly, the Ogwa Obi was also the place where ancient warriors gathered together to set out to war and where they returned to narrate their conquest. Thus, the need to preserve history more than the gods' wrath influenced my decision to offer to rebuild the Ogwa Obi. The day it was commissioned, I recalled a statement that was made by one of the Kingmakers; he said, *"Newton, now that you have washed your hands properly, you can now eat with the elders."*

The point of this trip down memory lane is to show that it is possible for development and progress to transcend religion. Nigeria is often torn between religions, and this has continued to breed and wreak havoc in many areas. We need to stop electing people based on what religion to which they subscribe. One's religion should remain one's private matter; it should play no role in the development of a nation or even an individual's expression of kindness.

• Restructuring

Restructuring has been making much news lately. When politicians talk about restructuring, what do they mean? Some people that have given restructuring a sovereign connotation which hints at splitting the country. In this case, the questions then are if the country is to be split, how many pieces are we talking about breaking it into? Who benefits and how does it improve the well-being of the people of Nigeria? In my personal opinion, we should look into what Mandela did in South Africa, where the country put together a peace and reconciliation committee because for there to be peace, there must first be active attempts at reconciliation.

The only way of getting out of the crisis of the three "R" is by getting to the root cause of these problems. Nigeria must not shy away from seeking help from outside the country if need be. We must seek for a lasting peaceful solution rather than our usual way of just dressing the surface without attending to the wound.

When I started these writings, I thought of recommending Kofi Annan because of his diplomatic disposition, integrity, and the fact that his first wife was a Nigerian, but regrettably, Kofi Annan passed away in August 2018, and I was distraught. Thus, I would like to use this opportunity to pay tribute to a wonderful African, who made the continent very proud for the eight years he served as the Secretary-General of the United Nations. May his soul rest in perfect peace.

Nigeria must seek for somebody with similar

stature and integrity to help mediate the peace and reconciliation talks. In doing so, we must remember the Northern Ireland crisis, which lasted almost three decades, was finally taken to a Good Friday agreement by American Senator, George Mitchell. It took him and his team many years to resolve the crisis, but most importantly, it was resolved.

People like Senator Mitchel, Kofi Annan, Desmond Tutu are difficult to find, but we must seek them out for the sake of unity and peaceful co-existence of the people of our land. We cannot continue to, at every stage or every crisis, sweep the dirt under the rug as we've been doing because one day, the rug will be overturned, and the dirt will return to haunt us indefinitely.

Nigeria, My Country, So Divided

The 2019 elected officials took on the reins of power with much anticipation in the air as people wondered what the next four years would look like for Nigeria and Nigerians. Would it be a change from the current status quo? Would it be business as usual? Or would we need to dodge for cover? I hope never the latter. I am, once again, caught up in memories that leave a lasting bittersweet taste as they remind me of the hopes and disappointments that come with being a Nigerian.

In the sixties, I was a young man who had just graduated from college in the United Kingdom. I remember how excited I was and very much in a hurry to return home to my beloved country, Nigeria. It was a nation that was united and emerging; one that was getting ready to compete with the rest of the emerging nations, and one that was expected to lead the rest of Africa. The prospects for Nigeria were endless. I recall telling my friends and mates in the United Kingdom before I return to Nigeria that if there were any continent that was likely to become another America, it would be the continent of Africa led by Nigeria because Nigeria had everything: human capital, fertile land for agriculture, oil and gas, gold, diamond, and more. It was easy to get caught up in my excitement as they wished me well and made plans to come to visit my country soon.

Another key part of the 60s was that it was also the era of space exploration. The continent of Europe had explored the space, the Americans and the Russians had landed on the moon. It was my greatest hope, as someone who loved adventure and discovering new things, that Nigeria would follow, and I would likely be part of that exploration. In my euphoria, I couldn't wait to get home to commence the adventure, so I decided to kick start it by driving my old car from London across Europe, over the Mediterranean sea in a ship and back on land to navigate through North Africa and across the Sahara to get to Nigeria. The journey lasted for two months and almost took my life. I remember vividly the moment the idea to drive across the Sahara took root in my mind. It was sometime around the end of the summer of 1964; I had just watched a video film made by my friends who had just come back from an expedition through the Balkans in East Europe. I was supposed to have been part of the expedition, but I had dropped out at the last minute because I was unable to raise the required £300 (three hundred pounds sterling) like the others to buy the equipment required for the journey. Upon their return, I watched the video clips, and I felt terrible.

Noticing my sad disposition, one of my closest friends at the time, Len Cocker, tapped me on the shoulder and said, "C'mon man, don't get emotional. We can do bigger things in the future."

I was not impressed and neither did I lighten up. The reason was simple; my studies were over, and I was preparing to return home to Nigeria. So, he jokingly suggested that we should drive across the Sahara. Intrigued, I asked him, "Is it really possible to drive through the Sahara?" He confessed that he had no idea but promised that we could find out. That was it for me. Although my friend decided not to embark on the journey after we found out it was possible but quite dangerous. I, on the other hand, was not deterred by the warnings. So, at the end of 1965, I did it, and that wasn't the last time I made the journey despite the challenges.

My return home was quite the experience. I was celebrated and became the desert warrior known as the first man to drive solo from the UK to Nigeria. This was to be the start of something great, or so I thought. I had barely settled in when the first military junta began following the 1966 Nigerian coup d'état which overthrew Prime Minister Alhaji Sir Abubakar Tafawa Balewa and made Major General Johnson Aguiyi-Ironsi the Head of the Federal Military Government of Nigeria. He too was soon overthrown and murdered in a coup in July of the same year. This followed a long list of more military coups, then a civil war that lasted three years. During that time, we went from four regions: the Northern, Western, Midwestern and Eastern region to 12 States, and now 36 States.

The military coup, the civil war, the killings, the divisions, and the bitterness that followed divided our country to a point of no return, causing the nation to degenerate into one huge ball of fractured pieces that may never fit quite well together again.

Every time I talk to my children and grandchildren, biological and non-biological, across the country, they have asked questions like, "will Nigeria ever get back to the good old days of my time?" I have found this question very useful, and most of us in the age bracket of the recipients of those good old days must provide the answers before we all go back to our Creator, and for us to do that we must all go back to the beginning.

The good Nigeria I grew up in gave me so much: a sound education, the ability to travel the length and breadth of the country and outside its shores; it also gave me hope. It felt like one nation, and I can say this after living in almost every part of the country. So, allow me to pose some questions to my generation and those who remain very much alive to provide the much-needed answers that this nation needs before we can begin a process of reconciliation and healing:

- What started the Western Nigeria crisis that was partly responsible for the military intervention in 1966?

- Why did the military overthrow themselves?

- Why the civil war; what happened to the Aburi accord?

- Why was the best election ever conducted in Nigeria annulled (12 June 1993)?

- Why is the military now wearing civilian clothes still in power?

• Why are we talking about Biafra almost 40 years after the civil war?

• How was Western Nigeria able to approach Oduduwa so diplomatically and even rule?

• Why did 11 states in northern Nigeria ask to belong to Sharia?

• What truly gave rise to Boko Haram and why are we still unable to tackle it?

• Why are people at the top very uncomfortable with the idea of Resource Control?

We the people of Nigeria must find answers to these questions, if not the unity which we so desire will continue to elude us. Our inability to find answers has prevented Nigeria from emerging into its full potentials 59 years after independence and leaving us still as a third world country.

Once again, I say there is a need for us to look back a little and review all the crises that have engulfed us since after independence in 1960, making it look as if we are not capable of governing ourselves. I noted it was time we prepared the platform for truth and reconciliation if we had any desire to embrace lasting peace and unity. Many conversations need to be had to aid or assist us in reviewing our mistakes, our bad deeds and bad judgments. We can learn something from South Africa, even if it means asking for help from outside the country. As mentioned earlier, people like Senator Mitchell, Desmond Tutu are difficult to find but not impossible. Barack Obama is an excellent choice because he displays a clear understanding of our unique problems and has shown himself capable of carrying the leadership mantle. So is Robert Mugabe for a different reason that may be open to debate.

I conclude by reiterating that the people of this country have been injured and fractured with unnecessary killings and division. The truth, therefore, must be told so that the process of healing and forgiveness can start, in so doing, a united and thriving Nigeria can return once more.

A Nation In Need of Intervention

With Nigeria turning 60, I'm full of mixed emotions as, on one hand, I'm happy to see this great nation reach such a milestone, and indeed it is a milestone not to have given way to war, natural disasters and more. On the other hand, I'm saddened by how far we have gone down the drain of bad leadership, corruption, and all things bad.

Some years ago, the then President of the United States, Barack Obama, made a video address to the Nigerian people in the run-up to the 2015 elections, asking them to shun violence. He said, *"all Nigerians must be able to cast their votes without intimidation or fear,"* and then called on all candidates to make it clear to their supporters that violence has no place in democratic elections. Fast forward to 2019 as the country prepared for another election, it felt as if the address, if made again, would have still been made relevant.

The issues that plagued the country leading up to the 2019 elections seemed even bigger; something we probably didn't think possible. Issues that, ideally, should be the driving force of development, like in so many countries. Our different cultures should be a source of attraction, not division; our oil should transform our nation into a better Dubai, and so much more, not divide us.

In his address, President Obama highlighted some issues that we had to address. The unfortunate thing, of course, is that some, if not all of these issues have been with us for decades, but we have continued to turn a blind eye to them hoping we can sweep them under the carpet. One crucial point he touched on was insurgency, which of course can be linked to Resource Control in some areas. He also mentioned free and fair election, which can be linked to the restructuring and resource control, especially the quest for control of the oil wealth.

You see I know what it means for a United States President to send a goodwill message to a country like Nigeria on the eve of a very crucial and challenging election like the one held in 2015. It must have been a wide-ranging diplomatic conversation amongst the friendly nations of the world that fear the slippery slope that Nigeria was about to enter. This message was well received by Nigerians at home and those in the diaspora. It was also viewed by hundreds, if not millions, of the entire black world.

That goes to show how much Nigeria is loved by particularly the black world. Therefore, the leaders and politicians of our country must not take the message for granted and brush aside its content as we engage in future elections because the unity of the country is even more at stake now with people feeling even more divisive than ever. I wrote about the "3R" threatening the development and the existence of Nigeria: Resource Control, Religion and Restructuring; I believe that until we are ready to address these 3Rs efficiently, the country will not advance.

Despite our disappointments and failures, many African countries still look up to Nigeria for leadership. Yet, we have never bothered to find out why the different systems failed before starting a new one. Thus, we cannot be talking about restructuring without looking at why we failed in the past. An example of how we have become too adapted to leap before looking is the collapse of Nigeria Airways before it even began. The government's plan to re-fleet the national carrier before the end of 2018 has been halted, as the Minister of State for Aviation, Senator Hadi Sirika, recently announced the suspension of the project. The suspension, which was greeted with absolute bewilderment across the country, came barely two months after the glamorous roadshow, that must have cost a fortune, was organized during the Farnborough Airshow in London where the name and the logo of the new airline was unveiled.

However, my question is, what happened to the last national carrier that was liquidated without any recourse to Nigerians with a debt of 43billion Naira? This amount was partly required to pay all outstanding claims of the ex-Nigeria Airways workers. We so easily dust our hands from 'failure' without dissecting the parts of it that could be useful learning for any future.

Under the topic on resource control, religion and restructuring, I had mentioned that the only way of getting out of the crisis of the "3R" is by getting to the root cause of these problems. I believe that as a country, we need not shy away from seeking help from outside if need be. It is possible that we are too buried in the dirt to see clearly, which may be preventing us from seeking a lasting peaceful solution.

It is interesting that so many countries still see Nigeria as a big brother and long to see what we can offer time and time again. I believe the love shown us by most countries in the world is what has sustained us thus far despite our failures and disappointments. We have suffered civil war, numerous military changes, two or three political dispensations, and still, we remain strong. But for how long? If we continue to take our resilience for granted, we will only live to regret that decision. We need help, and it's time we learn to seek it even if it's from the outside world without greed and corruption tainting good intentions.

PART III

CORRUPTION

"A system is corrupt when it is strictly profit-driven, not driven to serve the best interests of its people."

— Suzy Kassem

And

"To oppose corruption in government is the highest obligation of patriotism."

— G. Edward Griffin

Wasted Billions and The Economy: Don't Blame Corruption, Nigeria Is Cursed

Recently, I was on the phone with a dear friend, and as is customary for us, the conversation steered towards the state of the country. After our interesting conversation, I gave him a run-down of what I plan to write next, which is about the decay of the system and tracing it as far back as pre-independence. Then, my dear friend jokingly said to me that if I wanted people to read the article, I shouldn't mention corruption. He advised that I make our situation seem like a "curse" so that the traditional and religious institutions will have something to do by evoking the spirits behind the curse. It was a joke we both laughed over, but the words lingered on in my mind.

Hence, the choice of this title. However, I can't help but ask, are we cursed or just corrupt? Never mind the comments by the former Prime Minister of Britain about Nigeria being "fantastically corrupt." We can't possibly be described as such when we are yet to even agree on the scope of corruption: Can we classify theft as corruption? Nepotism? Our past president, Goodluck Jonathan, attempted to explain corruption to us when he announced that "stealing is not corruption," but that explanation didn't go down too well with many people. Therefore, the definition of corruption in the Nigerian context remains elusive.

Unlike corruption, curses are something we seem to be more familiar with, wielding it as a defensive or offensive weapon against our enemies. We saw this in action weeks ago when His Royal Highness, the Oba of Benin, publicly placed a curse on human traffickers and those assisting them. He cursed these people in response to the continued exposure of illegal migration and human trafficking in Edo State. With media reports of mysterious deaths and diseases following the curse, some seem to believe in its ability to bring around the desired improvement in curbing the menace. While we hope that is the case, we shouldn't hold our breath just yet since we live in a country where snakes and monkeys cart away with millions.

As we debate the possibility of a cursed or corrupt

nation, it is necessary to trace the country's downward spiral from a booming economy, with a currency that rivalled the dollar, to one that is continuously at the mercy of unstable exchange rates, international aid and foreign investors.

In our usual culture of keeping quiet and acting like nothing happened, we have failed to demand answers from key people over the failure of our industries. In the eighties, with four refineries and Nigeria's status as a leading oil and gas producer, we had the capacity to process refined commercial crude oil for domestic consumption and export. This was expected but hasn't been the case for many years because of the poor state of the refineries, despite the billions of naira that has gone into building and refurbishing these refineries. Consequently, the nation has become a major refined product importer with very negative implications for its economy. Moreover, it was revealed that Nigeria's refining capacity is one of the smallest compared to its peers.

There have been many talks on reviving the refineries, all to no avail. The most recent move by the Federal Government on the issue was to consider a policy whereby multinational oil and gas firms operating in the country would be compelled to build refineries in Nigeria. This might just be the best solution since we have proven unable to do it ourselves.

Another industry we ran aground and still struggling to revive is the Steel Industry. This is an industry that could have been the backbone of our nation because it would serve as a stimulus to national development and an economic boost to the industrial growth of any country. The idea of having a Steel industry was conceived in 1958 by the federal Government. At that time, preliminary market studies were carried out. These studies were initially directed towards the feasibility of establishing rolling mills. However, because of the growing awareness of the availability of iron ore in Agbaja, Udi, and other areas of the country, emphasis later shifted to establishing an integrated steel plant.

For most of the 1960s, the Federal Government invited and received proposals from foreign firms, including those from the UK, USA, Germany and Canada; most of these being on the feasibility of establishing steel complexes. At first, the efforts of the government did not yield significant result because they were based on the use of iron deposits in Agbaja and Udi, which were later found to be unsuitable for direct reduction.

However, by 1973, suitable iron ore deposit was discovered in Itakpe, Ajabanoko and Oshokoshoko; all in the region around Kabba-Okene-Lokoja – Koton Karfe axis, now in Kogi State. This was great news at that time and looked to be the beginning of Nigeria's industrial revolution. The discovery led to the Ajaokuta Steel Company, but along the way, it never kicked off as expected. Decades later, we are yet to own a thriving steel plant.

As far back as 1994, the Federal Government had spent over $10 billion to reach 98 percent completion, over 34 years, and would require another $2 billion to complete the remaining two percent of the plant. If operational, the Ajaokuta steel has the capacity to become a major producer of industrial machinery, auto-electrical spare-parts, shipbuilding, railways and carriages. The steel plant can provide direct employment for 10,000 technical staff and indirect employment for about 500,000, for unskilled upstream and downstream jobs if it is in operation.

There was also the case of our River Basin Authority that would have revolutionized the agricultural industry. Six River Basin Authorities were built for the supply of potable drinking water and irrigation. The irrigation was also to promote two seasonal cropping in the year, which would bring about food security in most of the dry land regions that have lost their capacity. This, however, didn't happen, and the communities that were made to settle around the Chad and River Basin Authorities were left stranded.

Another industry we once had at optimum capacity was the paper industry. In the 60s and 70s, the Federal Government established three Pulp and Paper Mills namely, Nigeria Paper Mill Limited (NPM) in Jebba, Kwara State; the Nigeria Newsprint Manufacturing Company Ltd (NNMC) in Oku-Iboku, Akwa-Ibom State; and the Nigeria National Paper Manufacturing Ltd. (NNPMC) in Ogun State. Two of the mills, NPM and NNMC, performed well in the 80s, which faded out paper importation during this period. Unfortunately, bad management, corruption and other factors did not benefit the industry in the long run.

It is believed that the nation is losing about N180 billion (Naira) from the non-performance of the three paper mills. Their non-performance also means that jobs that should have been created are lost to other countries. According to an article in The Nation Newspaper, this is also worsened by the fact the Federal Government spends N50 billion (Naira) on importation of paper annually.

Then there were the Vehicle Assembly Plants; we had six of those in the 60s. The plants were going to enable Nigerian companies to produce vehicles in the country as done in other parts of the world, which will, in turn, create jobs and boost the economy.

Another former glory was our three public institutions that cut across different sectors. In transportation, we had the Railway Corporation; in telecommunications, there was Nigerian Telecommunications Limited (NITEL), and in aviation, Nigeria Airways. In an era, when countries were expanding their infrastructure to be more sustainable and durable, we were losing ours. Now, as they enjoy the fruits of their labour, we work hard so that we can afford to travel to these countries and spend our hard-earned income, under the cover of vacations and tourism.

The mindboggling fact is that these failed industries have the potential to provide over 10 million jobs across the federation.

Globally, evidence abound in literature confirming a strong nexus between corruption and infrastructural decay. Evidently, it is not the absolute lack of funds that has caused infrastructural decay but outright mismanagement of funds. That is what is principally responsible for the level of infrastructural decay in Nigeria.

Up till 2011, Nigeria has remained among the top ten leading countries on corruption according to transparency international. But as supporters of Nigeria "being cursed" have pointed out, Nigeria is not the only corrupt nation in the world. In fact, they are quick to opine that many developed countries have corrupt leaders too, but these have managed to prosper still. If they are right, how do we then break this curse, or is our imminent doom inevitable? I choose to disagree because in my over 80 years on earth, I have been lucky to see life from different spectrums, and one thing holds true; a corrupt system can only produce after its own kind.

Therefore, until we start holding people accountable for their failures and stop blaming unseen forces, our problems will be far from over. Learning from our past mistakes, misconducts, and corrupt practices is paramount. There is no point starting over if we don't know why we never succeeded before.

Nigeria and Its Long History With the Fight Against Corruption

Corruption threatens sustainable economic development, ethical values and justice; it destabilises our society and endangers the rule of law. It undermines the institutions and values of our democracy. The effects of corruption are severe and widespread, and a larger number of our populace suffer its harmful effects most grievously, with the increasing levels of poverty and income inequality. But even worse is that corruption constitutes a threat to security as an enabler for crime and terrorism, as is alarmingly evident in the country today.

Corruption became a menace, such that the unique selling proposition of a battle against it excused and paved the way for military rule and dictatorship in young independent Nigeria. The very first coup of 1966 that plunged the nation into military rule, and eventually civil war, had corruption as one of the main reasons for staging the coup and the various coups that came after. However, rather than battle and eradicate it as promised, corruption seemed to have won the battle, as it ate deeper into the fabric of our society during these military dispensations. Eventually, the democratic dispensation was ushered back in, and the aspiring leaders chanted phrases like "no more business as usual," making promises, once again, to fight corruption. The theatrics were so convincing, some of us believed the infallible corruption might have finally met its match. Alas, we spoke too soon.

The anti-Corruption war in Nigeria has spanned several decades across different regimes and governments. In other words, from the military to civilian governments, every existing power always devises one form of mechanism or the other in the prosecution of this fight against this social menace. This fight in some way, even dates back to the pre-colonial era, as the various pre-colonial societies had systems in place preset to fight corrupt practices. For instance, my research reveals that the Yoruba Alaafin, who was the traditional head of the Yoruba society, stood to commit suicide or be banished on the event of abuse of his office. This act was to check the Alaafin from corrupt practices, and he was to ensure that his officials were also not corrupt. In the Igbo societies, for fear of any possible abuse of office, the political system did not repose authority on a single individual. In the North, the Emir was checked by the collective efforts of his officials and the Sharia Law.

Agencies like the first military-sponsored anti-corruption campaigns under General Murtala Mohammed called *"Operation Purge the Nation"*, to Shehu Shagari's ethical revolution, to Major General Tunde Idiagbon's *"War Against Indiscipline (WAI)"* under Gen. Muhammadu Buhari's military regime, later adjusted to *"War Against Indiscipline and Corruption (WAIC)"* by General Sani Abacha, had been established to battle corruption. The era of civilian governments also had their different anti-corruption mechanisms, like *"Economic and Financial Criminal Commission (EFCC)", "Independent Corrupt Practices and other related Crimes (ICPC)"*, among others.

However, the weaknesses of these institutions following their infection with the same vice they were to fight have made the fight against corruption more longwinded than many hoped. It is mind-boggling that after all these, we are still fighting corruption with no clue of how to win the battle. Many times, it almost feels like we have decided to live with it or accept peanuts. For instance, it is appalling how it is lauded as a major success in fighting corruption, the fact that some money stolen by private individuals and government officials were returned to the government from outside and within the country, when in fact, it is a very shameful situation.

Furthermore, some social critics will tell us that corruption is responsible for poverty, while others will say that poverty is responsible for corruption. Whatever the case may be, allow me to briefly describe what harm corruption has done to the nation and the psyche of the people all the way down the pyramid.

Over 50 years ago, western Nigeria was the first part of the country that started a television network and the slogan adopted for the station was "First in Africa". This was a few decades before apartheid South Africa established their own television station. Today, South African television networks are all over the continent even Nigeria needs the platform they provide to reach out to other parts of the country and the world. Their institutions, like DSTV, now employ millions. So where is Western Nigeria Television today, the first in Africa?

Then, there was NEC, which later became NITEL and was the first to establish a cable network that was also the first in Africa. Today, where's NITEL? There exists not a single telephone landline anymore. Another progress that has bitten the dust is Nigeria Airways; our national carrier started with 28 planes and was the pride of Africa. I recall flying from Bangui to Abidjan in the 80s and feeling very excited as I landed the airport and saw three Nigerian Airways planes set to fly to different parts of the world. It was one of my proudest moments as a Nigerian. Today, where is Nigerian Airways? Nigerians are now connecting the rest of the world through Kenyan Airways or Ethiopian Airways, institutions that started decades after Nigeria Airways.

I can go on and on to talk about our collapsed refineries and the fact that we are now importing refined products from countries to which we export the raw materials. Let's not forget the pathetic situation with our power supply. It is worthy to note that most of the countries enjoying uninterrupted power supply did not invest one-tenth of what we did into power generation. However, while these countries generate between forty to fifty thousand megawatts, we are still just generating under seven thousand megawatts. To put things into even more damning context, Norway produces 36,000 megawatts of electricity for five million people; Nigeria produces 7,000 megawatts for 200 million people. This means that the majority of our power source comes from Generators using petrol or diesel, which is expensive and does not benefit manufacturing in the country nor the environment.

Estimates indicate that over 90 percent of businesses and 30 percent of homes (I believe the figures are higher) have diesel-powered Generators. In Nigeria, diesel emissions from domestic generators surpass those from workplaces, trucks and buses, and pose greater risks to human health and the environment due to proximity to homes and prolonged duration of use.

I see no way our children and grandchildren will have the kind of developed nation we dreamt of and promised them if we do not eradicate corruption and bring people to account. Those countries that were in the same underdeveloped bracket with us some 50 years ago have moved on to become part of the emerging economies of the world and have successfully taken millions of their people out of poverty. With my eyes, I saw Dubai and many desert cities transform into world-class cities to compete with the West. They did so with oil money as well.

To the new generation of leaders seeking to lead this nation and give it a break from its usual handlers,

I challenge you. If you want to do better, you would need to find a way to contain corruption - a way of servicing our debts without crashing the economy. It is true that corruption is as old as man, but we have seen nations flourish despite corruption. They achieved this feat by putting in place structures that will deter corrupt practices, prosecute, and punish the corrupt.

Corruption Aka Giving Gifts

Each election year comes with much anticipation and anxiety. For me, mostly anxiety because it brings to mind 'corruption', even as we all match to cast our votes for whom we want to lead us. I often wonder, would the aspiring leader be picked on merit? Would the person be selected based on sentiments? Or would it be because the candidate has done a better job at buying peoples' vote? Many, like me, hope it would not be the latter or even the immediate former, but I have a few decades of experience to know not to be so hopeful. Still, I hope. The interesting part of the latter is how society has come to justify it as the act of giving gifts to electorates. *"It isn't bribery and corruption"* they say, *"it is appreciation."* Yes, a few bags of rice here, a few T-shirts, and don't forget the transport allowance the candidates distribute in a bid to appreciate their supporters.

We can laugh at the rhetoric in this instance. But having gone through the whole spectrum of professional life: rising from a fairly junior position in my organization to the very top, I have concluded that there is no way I can talk about corruption without being self-indicting. And as a Nigerian, hardly can you, in one way or the other.

This topic is culled from my autobiography, *Hunger for Power,* and aimed at the need for self-reflection. I don't think I would have gotten to where I am today if I wasn't involved in corruption, no matter how tangentially. But first, I want to talk about how corruption has become so embedded in our system and how it is even difficult to tell how it all started.

The interesting thing is that everyone talks about corruption. And while every one of us is involved in it, we somehow always manage to absolve ourselves, and that is why it is only getting worse. It runs the gamut from mere gifts, to the massive looting that we have today because people have not been able to come out openly to address the issue of corruption. I hope that by the time I am done with my stories, we will come up with some idea as to how to deal with corruption.

To begin with, it is pertinent to see how our affiliations have and continue to play critical roles in how pervasive corruption has become. We must all begin to confront corruption by considering how our culture plays a role; how our involvement with the quest for leadership in Student Union, Trade Union movement, Professional Unions, and other associations play a role. When you were affiliated with these unions, how did you conduct yourself and your affairs? A proper assessment will help you measure your corruption quotient.

The first story I will tell is about me giving, and the second story is about me receiving. When I got my gold pen, which I still have, and when Mr. Farrington, my boss at the time, asked me about my nice gold pen, I didn't tell him it was a gift from our client, and I didn't give it back because I didn't see it as wrong.

In Nigeria, it is customary to present a gift to your elders, superiors, and friends, especially when you need a favour from them or after the favour has been done to you. The colonial masters caught on and soon became adept at presenting gifts of Gin, clothing, and jewellery to our chiefs and kings. Unfortunately, with time, the magnitude of these gifts began to increase exponentially, and officials in positions of authority began to demand these gifts upfront rather than wait for the gifts to be offered. And thus, Nigerians unwittingly welcomed corruption into our business life. The challenge for us in my company then was; how do we make profit while delivering quality service to our clients and still compete effectively? In other words, how do we stay in business in a new Nigeria?

The fact was that things had changed dramatically since the colonial government handed over at Independence. When the colonial masters were there, once you did your job well, you got paid. If you did your job on time, you made your profit. You encountered problems only when you were not able to finish on time. That was only when they would hold on to your balance. But after they left, we began to see that in most cases, delaying your payment was often deliberate, either from the civil servants or the system that controlled the certification of those payments. So, what do you do?

That was where my problems started with my bosses from Europe because they had a policy. You must not do this, and even if you do, it must not be more than so, so and so.

Sometime in the 70s, we were on a foundation project for the extension of a popular hotel in Victoria Island, Lagos. I was mandated to negotiate the contract with the client. A final presentation was scheduled with the entire board of the client company. My friend, who was a board member, advised me to come with a gift for the board. On further probing, he suggested the sum of one hundred thousand naira, which at the time was equivalent to one hundred thousand pounds sterling.

I had a hard time convincing my Managing Director to play ball, but in the end, he reluctantly agreed. I could understand his reluctance because there was no guarantee that I would not be duped. On the day of the presentation, I attended the meeting, and after the technical presentation, the chairman whispered to me to present my gift formally. Not knowing how to do this, I began with a story:

"Mr. Chairman, distinguished board members, we have a saying in my place that, 'you do not pay homage to the king with an empty hand.' Please accept the offer of a small packet of kolanuts for this august meeting."

"Well, kolanuts are usually presented at the start of a meeting," one board member quipped, as the Chairman received the envelope from me.

"Let's see what you have here." And with that, the Chairman opened the envelope. After counting the money, he proceeded to share it; N10,000 to each board member. With only eight board members in total, he had N20,000 left. He looked at me, then counted N10,000 and offered it to me.

"No, sir; thank you, sir, but I cannot accept it. The kolanuts are for you."

"It is customary for the presenter of the kolanut to partake of it too," answered another board member.

With that, my spirited defence melted away like snow in the desert sun. I took my share of the money, thanked them and left. The next day I took the money to Mr. Farrington, my boss, and told him the story. He coldly asked me to return the money to the cashier and sign a new withdrawal form for N90, 000 as against the previous one of N100, 000.

"Damn," I thought. My boss could not even see the humour in this transaction. In the end, though, the board members were all gentlemen, and we were awarded the contract.

In a way, I had accepted the N10,000 as part of my "kolanut" and who would blame me. My salary at that time was N2, 500 a month. Imagine what that money could have done to the little bungalow I was building at that time. In my mind, I had said, "Let me show Mr. Farrington that I am transparent." That was why I mentioned it to Mr. Farrington. But

I was shocked when he said, "return it."

This act of gifting occurred in both directions. In our kind of business, we dealt with a lot of third-party vendors, and there were always those who showed appreciation for the business we gave to them. One such vendor was a Lebanese-Jew, who supplied us with reinforcement and structural steels for our projects.

One Christmas season, he came to the office and presented me with what appeared to be a solid gold pen. He must have known that I treasured good pens and that I collected them. I happily accepted the gift and thanked him for it. On the first week of resumption of work the following year, I was in Peter Farrington's office, and as usual, we were sharing holiday stories.

"Newton, you remember Sayeed, the steel supplier?" He asked.

"Yes, I do," I replied.

"He gave me a beautiful gold wrist-watch as a Christmas present last December whilst in London during the holidays. I decided to have it valued by a jeweller, and you cannot believe the value placed on it. At least twenty thousand pounds sterling!" Peter told me.

"Goodness me!" I exclaimed. "That is good for you. Congratulations."

"What, congratulations?" Peter queried. "I am going to return it to him. I cannot accept such an expensive gift."

I looked at Peter incredulously while a question raged in my head; "What is wrong with you? Somebody gave you a present you did not solicit for and which you had accepted. Now, you found out the worth, and you want to return it for being too expensive for your taste?" But I could not say that to him. Neither could I tell him that Sayeed had also given me a gold pen. I still have the pen till date but never had the courage to have it valued.

Corruption is responsible for poverty. It is the same corruption that makes it impossible for 60 to 70 percent of Nigerians to have access to potable drinking water. Corruption makes it impossible to have the kind of infrastructure we should have. The truth is that we have the money to do these things, but corruption has prevented us from getting them done, to make the lives of the populace better. So once again, I am forced to ask if we really want change or if we can handle the change that we need for our society to progress. Thus, this further begs the questions: How are our political elections conducted? Are the candidates elected based on merits or on what 'appreciation' we stand to receive? These are the most fundamental questions everyone should ask, for the essence of nationhood and democracy is embodied in these questions.

The Minimum Wage Debate: Contributing to the Endemic Corruption in Nigeria

I have always pondered why living wage matters should be between labour union and government. What is known today as the minimum wage syndrome started immediately after the abolition of slavery, particularly amongst the countries that harboured slaves. The minimum wage was, therefore, mainly introduced to stop the continuation of the practice. It came to be that if you must continue to keep the slaves in any employment, you must pay a minimum amount to them turning slaves into employees. By doing so, it became a political issue used between the government and the labour union to score points. In the same vein, you have what is known in today's employee-employer protocol as a collective bargaining arrangement. In this protocol, you have the right as the employer to hire and fire, and also a 'no work–no pay' understanding. Therefore, the right of the employee must be that *"if you want my service, you must be prepared to pay me a living wage."*

Employees must individually come to this knowledge of their right and be firm to demand a better wage for the services they offer. They also do not necessarily need to depend on a labour union to start or chart this course. Simply put, as an employee, if an employer offers you conditions that you don't think you can live on or terms that are not commensurate with the services you are required to offer, you turn down the job and look elsewhere. It is possible that given the rate of unemployment in the country, an employee may be tempted to take up a job that clearly will not meet his or her needs. No doubt, in turning down an offer, one may feel that he or she is the losing party because the employer can always look for the next candidate who may gladly take up the job with even lesser terms.

However, if every employee develops a mindset of dignity in labour and is willing to take the risk on turning down offers that don't meet their needs, rather than accept them for fear of remaining unemployed, their situation could substantially improve. This way, employers will be forced to offer more if they know that employees will not just take anything they dish out. If this is not done, we may continue with what we have today, which is very close to modern-day slavery, as against the dignity of labour.

Some time ago, I was at a social gathering, and also at the event was Adams Oshiomole, who was the President of the Nigeria Labour Congress (NLC) at the time. It was a very big event, and bottles of Champagne were being popped quite frequently. It so happened that at the time, there was also an impending strike over the minimum wage issue, and a funny scenario occurred at the event. Almost every time a bottle was popped, and it made a loud noise, Adams Oshiomole will shout *"there goes the minimum wage!"* I didn't understand the seriousness in the joke until I later found out that the amount being negotiated by the NLC was the average cost of a low-end bottle of Champagne, which ranged between N14,000 to N30,000.

Most of us retired or retiring former executives with over 45 years of working experience, who hired labour in the past, know that the drivers, the domestic staff, the security staff we have in our homes and offices, the Police and Custom officers at the checkpoints, the airline staff that issue boarding passes, the Press officers, and the NEPA officials that we employ can never survive on a pay of less than N100,000 monthly. But people take these jobs where they get paid meagre sums for fear of being unemployed and then begin to "innovate" ways to get something extra on the job. In the end, we create opportunities for corruption and dubious activities, bringing about a situation where these employees do not give their best to the jobs we hired them to do. After all, they are working for the wage the employer is paying and not what they can live on.

Thus, it is vital that we make a clear distinction between minimum wage and a living wage. Minimum wage, as I described earlier, is a concept that was used as a solution to prevent unpaid slave wages. It is not always the wage an employee deserves. In my opinion, the more appropriate concept that should be adopted is a living wage.

An individual who wants to employ a steward should be open to negotiating a wage the steward can comfortably live on. If this individual is not able to agree with the living wage suggested by the steward, he should look elsewhere or find someone else who is willing to accept his offer.

Paying employees what they deserve is one of the major steps to take in the restoration of the dignity of labour. Your driver who is given N5000 to fuel the car will spend N4000 in filling up the tank and pocket the change. The police and custom officers will mount roadblocks (sometimes unauthorized) to extort money from the road users. The domestic help will eat all your good food and send some home to their families. The press workers will demand their brown envelopes. They do all these because they have school fees to pay, rent to pay, mouths to feed, and have to fund their transportation to and from work, etc. For some of these employees, a salary of N100,000 will not be sufficient to take care of their responsibilities. So why must we keep fooling ourselves and hire such a person? Why must we look the other way and allow corruption to develop from the bottom – up?

Most of these categories of workers know that his or her boss is on a salary of a little over N200,000; yet is able to afford to build a house worth over N50m and drive a car worth N20m. Some of these employers include faith workers (Pastors and Imams) who misappropriate funds which have been given to the Church or Mosque as personal offerings from members of the congregation. These employees also know that these bosses make millions monthly outside the constraints of their employment, which is why the employees thought process is usually skewed towards the unfairness of his employer.

We have gotten used to not asking questions about the shady sources of income that we see within our communities. Strangely enough, a lot of Nigerians aspire to be like that wealthy man or woman with untraceable sources of income. This reminds me of a funny story I once heard about a Nigerian businessman and a European businessman. The European businessman was asked how he acquired his wealth and became successful. He answered the question with facts only: He mentioned his successful real estate business, a vibrant investment portfolio, amongst many other concrete sources. When it was the turn of the Nigerian businessman to answer the question, he puckered his lips, and with a wide grin on his face, he exclaimed, *"Na God oh!"*

The endemic corruption in the country cannot be stopped systematically if we don't review the wages offered to our employees. In the past, corruption was only present in top positions, but today, it is spread across the whole pyramid scheme. Somehow, this plague of institutional corruption has trickled down to the bottom of the pyramid. This must not be allowed to continue. Therefore, the time to restructure the employer-employee pay arrangement starts now, not tomorrow. The labour movement must rise in support of this and also stop politicizing the process. If the bar continues to be lowered, it will come crashing down and the consequences for the country will be disastrous.

Fighting Corruption in Nigeria

When the white man crossed the sea to our lands, they came bearing gifts for the sole purpose of making the inhabitants more welcoming and susceptible to their plan of world domination and resource control. The gifts were meant to clear the path for them and so it did for the most part. I have always seen this as a different kind of corruption – an imported kind that made its way into Africa through the colonial masters. However, I must state that giving gifts, on their part, was not a new innovation. This followed our existing traditional way of presenting gifts to people of higher social status when we visit them. Ours, however, was as a sign of respect, not manipulation.

This system of giving gifts continued well into the colonial rule as many benefited from it, mostly in the upper class with the likes of permanent secretaries, kings, and queens. The gifts also trickled down to the middle class: the police, customs, judiciary system, and so on. Although, for the middle class, the colonial masters kept a sharp eye on things to ensure that things remained under control by quickly fishing out those living above their income. A way of saying, "be corrupt but not too corrupt," so the upper class can be better fed.

A keen look at Africa's history will show that the administrative corruption that is ubiquitous on the continent is actually "an alien culture". Pre-colonial Africa had a system founded on strong ethical values usually rooted in spirituality, but with the outcome of ensuring social justice and compliance.

The Yoruba culture of western Nigeria had the Oyo-mesi, which was the king-making body that served as a check against the abuse of power by the Alaafin (the Oba) or the King of Oyo. The Alaafin was constrained to rule with caution and respect for his subjects. If he were proven to have engaged in acts, like a gross miscarriage of justice for personal gains, the Oyo-mesi would present the king with an empty calabash or Parrot's eggs as a sign that he must commit suicide. According to tradition, he could not be deposed; thus, he must die.

In the Igbo acephalous society, the absence of any singular form of authority placed leadership with the people. Titled Chiefs sat together to address the more difficult issues of governance, and there is a saying among the Igbo that a "titled man does not lie." If one wanted to hear the truth or to be granted pristine justice according to the prevailing standards, he or she only needed to get the impeccable body of titled men to hear the case in question.

All these systems were eventually corrupted and destroyed by the colonialists. The gifts to these traditional leaders with promises of more, for them to get their people to do the white man's bidding, began the downward spiral of effective systems of justice. This eventually became the norm in our nation and most of Africa. Thus, colonialism introduced systemic corruption on a grand scale across much of sub-Saharan Africa. The result is what is rampant across Africa today: conspicuous consumption, absence of loyalty to the state, oppressive and corrupt state institutions, to mention few.

At first, even though the practice was there, it did not extend to the private sector. However, when the British colonial masters gave up control, other foreigners like the Egyptians, Lebanese, Chinese, Middle Easterners, and Central Europeans came with their own brand of corruption. This brand of corruption effectively converted a country like Nigeria into a "fantastically corrupt nation," as described by David Cameron.

During the colonial control, I recall that there was something called the "ten percentiles", which meant that when contracts or jobs were awarded, 10 percent of the profit and not more, would be set aside for top government officials. These top government officials in those days were then known as "ten percentiles" because that was how they got their wealth.

Many years back during a negotiation process involving a big foreign firm that my company was hoping to work with on a project. They had done a number of projects in Nigeria; so, they were quite familiar with some of the workings of our government officials. This was a massive contract and a top manager from the company was in the country handling the negotiation process. Due to the nature of the contract, this company was in negotiations with three different levels of government institutions. At each meeting with one level of government, this manager, who happened to be a good friend of mine, would be asked if he made any provisions for them. To this, he always assured the government officials that he had made a 10 percent provision for them.

He had mentioned this 10 percent provision to all three levels of government involved in the negotiation. When it was time for the first down payment to be made, they discovered that each level of government wanted 10 percent full, and not a part of it. He had expected to share the 10 percent amongst the three levels. When my friend found out that he had to pay 30 percent to the three institutions from their revenue, he had a heart attack, as it dawned on him that if he collected the money and didn't pay the 30 percent, his project was in trouble. He died not too long afterwards, and the contract never saw the light of day.

As if the 10 percent wasn't bad enough already, things got even worse. With the combination of the new brand of corruption brought in by all the nationals mentioned above, there was no more limit on the 'tithe or kick-back'. Thus, we started going as far as looting the treasury, and the resultant effects were:

- The hospitals meant to be built were never built, turning all of us into sick Nigerians, mentally and physically.

- The educational institutions were no longer funded, so while we got some form of education, there was no learning.

- Infrastructures were no longer built, and those that were eventually built were poorly done, making it difficult to address the issue of poverty alleviation.

Moreover, we are so carried away by the prospect of political power-sharing; a philosophy that, in my opinion, has only led Nigeria to where it is now. A country where no one works for its collective good, which tends to benefit everyone but are only focused on their numerous enclaves or self. This only promotes another bout of corruption and disjointed development.

Over the past few decades, the biggest threat to our country's emergence and development has been our inability to fight corruption. Particularly worse now that corruption is fighting back, and almost defeating all attempts that have been made by previous governments. For over 50 years, the different governments that have ruled, military or civilian, have vowed to stamp out corruption from the system knowing the damage it has done to the nation and its citizens. These governments have ended up overwhelmed by the fight, and in most cases, given up the fight, accepting defeat and becoming part of it by default. And there goes the saying that if you cannot beat them, join them. For goodness sake, therefore, let these politicians, either in Agbada or uniform, look for another slogan and stop fooling the Nigerians, because the slogan, "Fight Against Corruption" has been immensely overused. It is our collective responsibility to work for a better nation; and thus, I hope that someday we will eventually start to get it right.

Fighting Corruption In Nigeria: Mission Impossible?

As stated previously, systematic corruption, as it is practised today, wasn't the innovation of the black man even though we have continued to suffer because of it. My line of thought was in no way to exonerate us from any blame but to show just how widespread corruption is in our world. It was also to set the tone for the rest of my thought that seek to unceremoniously yank away the blindfold that may be preventing us from seeing that many nations have still managed to build a strong economy in a 'corrupt world'. I pointed out that colonialism introduced systemic corruption on a grand scale across much of Sub-Saharan Africa, but our overwhelming penchant for it has led to the state of underdevelopment of the country.

It must be known that there is no squeaky-clean

country in the world. The corruption perceptions index (CPI) is used to rank countries and territories of the world based on how corrupt their public sector is perceived to be. In a points system that ranges from 0 (the most corrupt) to 100 (the cleanest), Denmark with 88 points is the least corrupt or cleanest country, and Nigeria with 27 points ranks 144th in a total of 180 nations and territories for 2018. So, we are in the bottom 20 percent. This is definitely not a good thing, given that this index largely governs the response of the business world to our calls for foreign investment into our economy.

In a world that is fast becoming a global community, it is increasingly impossible for Nigeria to become insular, given our penchant for all that is foreign. However, it is ironic that though we love so much of the good life, we cannot produce much that is good. The Nigerian internal market is such a huge one given our population of over 189 million. If we could concentrate on creating quality goods and services that are consumed locally, our economy will be in the stratosphere. And so will our social services, our infrastructure, our schools, and our health services. Our health care delivery system would be world-class, given the quality of doctors we produce. And our manufacturing would be comparable to those of the industrialized nations.

A close study of the world's corruption index reveals that countries with CPI below 40 points have weak economies, tottering social services, elevated levels of poverty and wealth inequality. This is not accidental or conspiratorial marginalization by the industrialized nations, which is often the normalized excuse for abject failure. This is the price of corrupt and ignorant public sectors that formulate repressive and disruptive policies that are meant to benefit cronyism and perpetuate the ruling class. So, how did Nigeria, with its abundant human and natural resources, get into this club of failed states? Expanding on the brief account I had provided in my previous writing, let's take a closer look at our historical past.

Traditionally, Nigerians exhibit a huge sense of gratitude to each other in their communities. So, typically, every act of kindness or service right from ancient times was rewarded by gifting, sharing, or reciprocity. However, a different approach was adopted if one needed a favour from a constituted authority, such as a king or the community head. You would have to precede your supplication with a gift presentation that is meant to recognize his position of influence and not seen as a means of currying favour. The king would accept the gifts, share it with you, or present his own welcoming gift for all to partake, even when he rejects your entreaties because he could never be indebted to you. When the colonialists came, they adopted this tradition in their dealings with the kings and traditional rulers. They even extended it to acts that required the silence of the king in matters that would have otherwise necessitated his disapproval. A lot of internecine wars were fought over such matters, and the Nigerian kings lost those wars. So, the people began to see the white man's gifts as a means of buying the kings acquiescence. And as the white men conquered territories, they established their administrative controls, education, and governance.

To fund the government, the colonialists introduced the principle of taxation at all levels. This was strange to the indigenous people who were used to executing projects with free communal labour and feasting from contributed produce as compensation. Taxation, therefore, was alien to the people, poorly understood, and seen as a tool of suppression by the colonialists, who became thoroughly feared and hated. The people evaded taxes in droves and were also caught and jailed in large numbers.

Jailing people was also alien to our culture. In medieval times, our people rarely broke the laws. The most common infraction was stealing, but that too was of spartan occurrence and thieves were so easily caught and publicly shamed. Once in a long while, murder was committed, and the punishment was banishment from your kingdom. Such banishedpeopleeventuallydiedlonelydeathsindistant lands or no-man's land. There were no jails before the colonialists came. So, in those new eras, going to jail was something the people needed to avoid at all costs.

Our 'western educated' nationals who found themselves in the administrative offices with the colonialists saw their new status as symbols of authority over their kindred. Hence, expecting to be courted and revered by anyone that required their difficult-to-accomplish services of any kind. The popular TV series, *"Ichoku"*, which portrayed the travails of a corrupt Court messenger in the colonial times, starkly depicted the anguish of the ordinary Nigerian in his quest for justice or escape from the long arm of the law.

The ordinary Nigerian saw himself as a victim of the occupation force, the colonialist. He must, therefore, seek co-operation from his fellow brother, Nigerian in authority, to navigate the strange and perilous world of the white man. And so, the word bribery entered our lexicon and legal codes. Unfortunately, the nationals in the justice ministry that were charged to fight and prosecute this were the first line of cooperating kindreds for the hapless citizens. But as typical Africans, they were not offering money but gifts. Offering money was seen as bribes, but gifts were forms of appreciation. Bribe taking was criminalized, a taboo, and shameful act.

Life continued that way until well into our independence, at which time we assumed full responsibility for our collective destiny. I believe that because of inadequate education and public enlightenment, the people poorly understood taxation, governance, and the rule of law. We saw these institutions as coercive instruments of colonialism. Consequently, in our own governance, we failed to strengthen them, as we equally got carried away with control of our affairs and the apparent wealth in the system. It was then easy for politicians to believe that they need not work hard to govern adequately. The oil boom of the middle sixties and seventies placed so much money in the hands of the civil servants, who could not resist the temptation to devise ways of dipping their hands into federal and regional coffers.

At this point in our development, our First Republic politicians and top civil servants encouraged the people they served (especially the foreign businessmen) to always come back to show the traditional appreciation for services and help rendered. These appreciations were in various shades; paid vacations, company share allotments, expensive gifts, and monetary gifts, though seldom. The Europeans then mastered the Nigerian art of gifting and used it effectively. With time, our people, ever so ingenious, became adept in agreeing on what the appreciation would be pre-contract; thus, heralding the arrival of the era of kickbacks.

It did not take long for the lower and middle-level civil servants to understand what their bosses were up to. They devised their own system, rooted in frustration, of collecting kickbacks. In their own case, it was more of a mixture of pay it forward, as the sums demanded were relatively low. Such methods included vanishing project or subject files, and delays in the production of cheques on approved payments.

On a personal experience, I had gone to FCDA Abuja, in the late 70s to pursue a payment due to the company I worked for at the time. It was a Friday, and I had arrived Abuja with the first flight to return that evening. After securing the Minister's approval (with whom I had an earlier appointment), my file was moved to accounts for cheque writing and disbursement to me at about

9.15am. Two hours later, while I was still waiting to pick up my cheque, I noticed that some people who came in after me were walking out with their cheques. On advice from a concerned staff who sympathized with me, I went to see the senior accountant, who demanded N30,000. I refused to pay that and instead offered him N5,000, which he rejected, so I left his office. An hour later, I was still waiting. My sympathetic staff-friend informed me again that perhaps I should go back to the Minister. She advised that since the Minister would soon be departing to the Mosque for Friday Jumat Prayers, I should position myself by the exit to catch his attention. This I did, and truly, the Minister was shocked to find me there. I told him that I was yet to collect the cheque. He was furious and ordered the finance director to produce my cheque within minutes.

I eventually picked it up, got into my car to head for the airport only to find the senior accountant flagging me down. In response to what he wanted, he reminded me of the money he demanded earlier. I looked at him for a while with incredulity but remembering that I would certainly need him again and again, I gave him ten thousand naira. I believe many Nigerians can relate to my experience in one way or the other from either side of the spectrum.

Furthermore, corruption can also be seen in the way the nation's police force run's like a private enterprise. Some time ago, it was reported that over 75 percent of our police force is engaged in the provision of private third-party security services all over the country. That leaves just about 25 percent of the force to be engaged in actual police duties. The outcry that rightly greeted this revelation prompted the directive from the presidency instructing the Inspector General of Police (IGP) to withdraw all those police officers engaged in extra-curricular duties. But that directive has not been fully implemented. This, amongst other reasons, has intensified the call for state police. This call should not be ignored; we need state policing, with federal oversight, and a federal investigative bureau that is modelled after the USA's FBI, charged with securing our democratic institutions. The system we have now is modelled after that of the British. Due to our diversity, and thanks to the military governments of the past, it has not worked. Besides, our current population, which will be in the region of 200million in a few years is too populated to be managed by a central police force. The police force must be decentralized, just like our courts.

Summarily, it is necessary to establish ethical institutions that will investigate breaches of ethics and codes of conduct in government at all levels, including the presidency - no sacred cows. With the broad definition of corruption and some of the stories narrated, it must be clear to the discerning mind that the fight against corruption cannot all be about catching and prosecuting those who embezzled public funds. The apprehension of these people will not end kickbacks or pay it forward; it would not end tribalism, or cronyism, or mediocrity. Neither would it improve the economy, nor service delivery, nor social services. You cannot apprehend everyone that is compromised, for that matter. But good governance will do all of the above, including the elimination and reduction of public funds embezzlement.

Good governance would ensure that the right people, who are ethical, capable, qualified, and experienced, are appointed into positions of authority. It would ensure that the right policies are put in place for the benefit of the country, and not to favour cronies. Good governance would ensure the rule of law exists in all aspects of our lives. It would ensure that the institutions that support democracy are established, adequately funded and strengthened to perform their oversight functions.

Ridding Nigeria of Corruption

It is essential to distinguish between conducting an election and deriving the essence of such an election. In many cases in Africa, elections are conducted in democratic nations, and the people vote, but the essence of the election is often missing. Thus, the people end up feeling like there was no election at all. This happens when the greater majority of the voters do not have a free and genuine choice between the candidates. Even when there exists a genuine choice of candidate, voters are often manipulated with gifts or threats to vote for the "chosen candidate" of the "powers-that-be". No doubt, the country conducted elections, but in many of them the elections are not competitive, or the electoral situation is compromised.

Reflecting on the 2019 elections, though saddled

with many flaws, yet I couldn't help but be impressed with the level of political participation that was displayed during the entire campaign and election. Despite the many reoccurring challenges that affected voter's turnout in some regions and encouraged apathy in some others; it is obvious that Nigerians are beginning to pay more attention to the essence of the governance of Nigeria.

Therefore, now more than ever, this is highly imperative because we must admit that Nigeria with its many potentials and impressive human resource, is a failed state. This is not a derogatory statement, but one based on factual pieces of evidence, many of which I provided in my previous pieces. If we are seeking solutions to our problems, we need to first and foremost understand what our problems are. Secondly, we need to recognise that our leaders have no clue on how to proceed. For you cannot fight a modern war with medieval implements. Therefore, the question is, how do we proceed to correct our bearings?

Nigerians are known to be the proud people of Africa, and who still recoil at the thought of being second best; these two reasons ought to be the rallying cry to action. A cry to rise up and fight the scourge of bribery and corruption, which has consumed this nation. What is left is for it to break the country into pieces. Some people might say, "all well and good, let's go our separate ways; we will then be better off." However, that cannot be achieved unless it is a coordinated break up. And if we can coordinate a controlled break-up, then we are much more capable of modifying a restructuring of the political, economic, and social fabric of our dear nation.

A country with a strong democratic institution will have good governance. Such a nation will also forge a strong economy. Good governance is not unattainable. It is simply doing things the right way, following due process, with a transparency of actions for the public good. It is the ultimate practice in excellence that has its roots in patriotism and civics. It ensures that everyone accepts accountability for his or her actions. Good governance ensures that checks, fraud alerts, and robust audits of our financial systems, fiscal policies, and the economy are deployed at all levels. Consumer protection watchdogs will be needed to protect the public from unethical practices and price gouging by the private sector.

The good news is that these institutions are largely in place in this country. However, the bad news is that they are completely emasculated by incompetence and inadequate funding by those intent on their failures to advance their hideous plans.

A lot of hearts must be fluttering at the sight and sound of restructuring because they are worried at the likely loss of power and privilege to dominate and pillage. But also, a lot more hearts will be beating the drums of support because they can see themselves in control of the supposed new order, where the states regain control of their affairs in the mould of the federal government. These two groups will be wrong.

The solutions to all of the above-stated ills and more lie within the core of the problems, in plain sight. As it stands today, every Nigerian, in living out his or her life, is his or her own government. Everyone provides his or her own electricity, water, school supplies, hospital supplies, community roads, security, and housing. When was the last time anyone turned the taps in his home to receive water from the public mains anywhere in Nigeria? Even Lagos State recognised this, but in the most callous decision any government can unleash on its people, it cashed in on this travesty. The State proceeded to impose a levy on all who have boreholes in their homes.

Many Nigerians go out of their way to buy sports utility vehicles, not because it's their choice, but as the solution to the bad roads they drive on. They don't see it worthwhile to complain to the government as they are ashamedly aware that government services do not exist in their lives. And it is precisely for this reason that the public servants and politicians are stealing us blind; to be able to provide these services to themselves even in retirement!

I recall that many years ago, the World Bank announced its 25-year target and introduced a model for countries to implement for a sustainable water system by the target date. The system was designed and supervised by the bank. Each country selected received aid in cash and kind from the World Bank to ensure that inaccessibility of potable drinking water became a thing of the past for all its citizens. Nigeria was a beneficiary of this project, and I was privileged to be among the committee that was formed under the Obasanjo administration to implement this World Bank project.

Unfortunately, the efforts by the committee, which was made up of both civil servants and non-civil servants like me, were marred with bureaucracy, diversion of the World Bank-provided funding, and much more.

Decades later, Nigeria still doesn't have potable

drinking water for all. Instead, we rely on our poison water, also referred to as "pure water, and sinking boreholes.

Another issue we seem to have come full circle over is that of living wages and the role of government. The latter, in Nigeria, must be to create and sustain the enabling environment for secure, economic growth while providing affordable social services to its citizens. In return, the citizens (inclusive of the government) are expected to fund these services through a combination of taxes and bill settlements. To make governments at all levels relevant again is the restructuring I am talking about here.

Such restructuring of the instruments of governance will involve the strengthening of our democratic structures. This is meant to ensure the rule of law, sustain ethics, checks and balances, and above all demonstrate trust, transparency, and confidence in the society. The good news is that these structures already exist; we only need to learn how to make them work for the common good.

We will only fight bribery and corruption with the deployment of a plethora of tools and methods. The age-old method of catching a thief is not enough. We must make it difficult for stealing to occur.

You cannot steal what you cannot see. Hence the push to a cashless society is both good and must be sustained to fruition. But then we must also be ready to train our financial inspectors and law enforcers to recognize internet frauds and stay one step ahead of the criminals.

The rule of law is pivotal to this fight. No one, not even the President shall be above the laws of the Federal Republic of Nigeria. Everyone has to be held accountable, especially those who provide goods and services. The power of the taxpayers must be recognized and respected; they are the electorates for goodness sakes. Democratic structures meant to ensure probity and ethics will ensure good governance and institution of excellence in administrations at all levels. Cronyism and nepotism must have no place in our society.

What I call the "in-opportune" costs of bribery and corruption is so huge. If these sums of money are left in our economy, these will ensure that we pay living wages to hardworking Nigerians. It will, in turn, unleash a vibrant economy that will get us into the league of world top economies. This march will take time, we must understand. And if we do understand, then we cannot afford to continue with the politics of tearing down the accomplishments of the past. Rather, we should build on that which is good. The over-arching goal here is to build this nation, regardless of our politics and ideologies. We haven't got another nation to call ours.

PART IV

LEADERSHIP AND POWER

Discerning the difference between a Dictator and a Leader is quite easy. The former cannot help but see 'leading' and 'serving' as stark contradictions that by their very nature are utterly incompatible. The latter can't tell the difference."

— Craig D. Lounsbrough

Leadership and Legacy

There is such a fascination with leadership and the legacy a leader leaves; many reasons propel people to attempt to become leaders. Many become obsessed with the mechanics, styles, and personalities, however, what is conspicuously absent is the thinking underpinning the politics of leadership. The integrity of nations, be it at the local or international levels is inextricably linked to not only leadership techniques but the reasons why people want to be leaders, which begs the question who are leaders and why are they leading? On this, I mulled over one of my trips to Paris, where I delivered a lecture on leadership at the University of Schiller, as part of the 2018 graduation ceremony of the University. The lecture was succeeded by numerous questions and comments but the underlying theme of the many queries was centred on the issue of youthful patriotism and how different the concept is now compared to the era of Martin Luther King, Nelson Mandela and many great leaders who started their fight for a better society in their youth. There was such great hope for many then that the tomorrow's leaders would do better since ***"the youth of today are the leaders of tomorrow."***

Many decades later, we are still quoting that famous mantra to ignite hope for a better future in us. The popular quote is one that I have heard often in different settings to either motivate young people to be more responsible for their future or to admonish the older generation for not being inclusive and leaving enough good examples for the youth to emulate. Regardless of why it is being used, if the youth of today are indeed the leaders of tomorrow, can we then rest easy that the future is in safe hands. As I concluded my lecture on leadership in the auditorium filled with soon to be graduates, undergraduates and the university's faculty leaders, I enjoined every youth present to ask themselves this question: How prepared are we to lead?

You see, there is hardly any human being alive that does not desire to be remembered positively as one who made an impact. In other words, there is hardly anybody on earth who does not wish to leave a legacy, preferably a positive one. However, not many are prepared to pay the price that such feat demands. We forget that legacy, though retrospective, must be built in the present moment with every choice we make, every decision we make and every action we carry out.

Many in the position of leadership seem to have forgotten that legacy isn't about building monuments to be remembered by, but the impressions we leave in the minds of those we lead based on our achievements, not promises. People remember what but they also remember who. We remember that infrastructures were built across the North from the revenues reaped from the groundnut pyramids. We remember how revenues from cocoa were used to facilitate free, quality education in the West. We also recall that the proceeds from palm oil and coal were used to build landmark infrastructures in the East. Yes, we remember what, but we also remember the men who built them. All over the world, young people are at the centre of societal interactions, especially in this age of globalization and modern technology where people are connecting worldwide as never before.

Another popular quote says, "Nothing ventured, nothing gained." Did we learn nothing from the generation that explored the space, the moon and set us on a course to conquer mars? Have we forgotten so quickly the lessons passed on from the generation that triggered the women liberation and civil rights movement? That was the generation willing to risk all for a nation they believed could be.

Do we still have leaders who can inspire change and cause a revolution? Sadly, I don't see any standing amongst my mates even though they seem unable to relinquish power at the 11th hour. Yet, I also wonder if those they will be relinquishing power to have what it takes to lead right.

My queries take nothing away from the amazing feats that young people have accomplished all over the world and particularly in my beloved country, Nigeria. Despite offhand comments by "he who shall not be named" about Nigerian youths being uneducated, unwilling to work and dependent on revenue from oil to survive, we keep seeing many young people counter such claims continually with their innovations and hard work.

However, leadership demands that in all our innovations and hard work, we work towards something that will do more than line our pockets but that which will benefit many. Nigerian youths from time immemorial have been contributing their quota towards national development. The likes of Sir Tafawa Balewa, Sir Ahmadu Bello, Chief Obafemi Awolowo, Dr. Nnamdi Azikwe, and Herbert Macaulay fought tooth and nail in their youth to deliver the political independence we all enjoy today as a nation. Thus, borrowing from the words of a man I admire, President John F. Kennedy, I implore our Nigerian youths, *"Ask not what your country can do for you; ask what you can do for your country."*

Being patriotic towards the nation is everyone's responsibility, for without us, there is no nation and without a nation, we will be lost – strangers in another man's land. The youth forms a significant part of the nation and being patriotic should be one of the major responsibilities of the people. Today, we enjoy freedom in heritage; this freedom came as a result of the sacrifices by the freedom fighters who were ready to die without a second thought to the activities that happened during the struggle for freedom and the amount of bloodshed that took place, so that we, as a country, can enjoy relative peace. Instead of bemoaning the failures of past generations, I think it's time we accept the fact that we need to shoulder the responsibility of becoming the redeeming generation for many reasons.

One of such reasons is that the youth of today will inherit the nation tomorrow; thus, if the youth do not become involved in making our nation better, they may not receive a nation worth inheriting. Another reason is, the nation built by today's youth will be the nation they will pass along to their own children, and if today's youth wish for their children to have a better Nigeria, the youth of today must protect and defend the nation by supporting our country's greatness and working to make her even better.

A journey of a thousand miles, they say, begins with a first step. So, as leaders of tomorrow, how prepared are you to break barriers and enter new frontiers? Preparation will be a first step in the long journey that is leadership.

In Search of Another Mandela, The Leader Who Led: A Mirage Or Possibility?

I laid half-awake in bed at three o'clock in the morning. Darkness enveloped my room at the Nelson Mandela Gardens, Asaba, Delta State; rubbing my eyes, I drowsily walked over to the window and peeked through, it was still dark outside, except for the lights that lit up the streets, and the airport was quiet in the hours before dawn. It was late June 2018, just a few weeks before the centenary anniversary of Nelson Mandela. As his name flashed through my mind, I found myself now fully awake, consumed by these words at once exhilarating and daunting:

"A new world will be won not by those who stand at a distance with their arms folded, but by those who are in the arena, whose garments are torn by storms and whose bodies are maimed in the course of the contest."

- **Nelson Mandela** (in a letter to Winnie Mandela,

written from Robben Island, June 23, 1969).

I sat comfortably on a chair in the darkness of my room reminiscing about the great benefits of good leadership, as Africa and the entire global community prepared for the celebration of Nelson Rolihlahla Mandela, which climaxed July 18, 2018. Many thoughts raced through my mind, but the one that stood paramount was the necessity for us to look north and south, east and west to find another Madiba because if only a small percentage of Africa can be like Madiba, the world and our continent will be a better place.

Using Nigeria as a relatable example, our past leaders have moral compasses pointing in the complete opposite direction of that of Mandela. Thus, I often think: If we have made it this far with questionable and selfish leaders, imagine how much further in the right direction we can go with leaders who possess half of the character traits of Mandela; leaders who truly lead.

With the continent surrounded by a plethora of unremarkably corrupt leaders, one's judgement can easily be clouded by the pain and disappointment that comes with losing a leader of such great repute. However, I will, as much as possible, be objective. Some people might not agree with my train of thought, but as someone who has been around for decades and successfully navigated my way to a peak position in one of Nigeria's top corporations, I daresay I have more than enough facts to back my theory that we lack good leaders in our society.

Although much damage has already been done, we still have a chance to right our wrongs and steer this country in the direction towards prosperity. However, before we can achieve this, we must re-evaluate our priorities, our character, and what we stand for in general. As the great Malcolm X once said, *"A man who stands for nothing will fall for anything."* That being said, can we all agree that we need to make some changes. Luckily for us, we don't have to look too far outside our continent to find a great leader to emulate.

Thus, I would like to highlight some key leadership qualities of Nelson Mandela, in hopes that our next generation of leaders can match or surpass them.

- **An Acute Level of Focus:** Nelson Mandela became an activist in the university when he aligned with both black and white activists who were also involved in the fight against racial discrimination. When apartheid was introduced in 1948, his alliance with the ANC grew stronger, and he was one of the people at the forefront of the fight against this.

During the fight against apartheid, he was convicted of treason and sentenced to life imprisonment. One would think that would break him and cause him to lose focus of his mission, especially being jailed in isolation and had to undertake the grueling work of pounding rocks into gravel, which is enough to make any man lose his mind or give up, but Mandela stayed laser-sharp focused. During his time in prison, his popularity grew around the world, and upon release in 1990, he immediately began negotiations to end apartheid in South Africa. Not deterred, his laser-sharp focus on the goal finally paid off, in 1994, for the first time, a black man was allowed to run for the office of the President of the Republic of South Africa. Nelson Mandela, backed by the ANC, won the election and continued to fight for his people. Nelson Mandela's fight against apartheid lasted for 42 years. Such level of focus for that length of time, despite all odds, is rare and is one of Nelson Mandela's finest qualities worth emulating.

- **A Will to Forgive:** When I was a younger man, I was quite stubborn. Very opinionated and head strong. It was due to this strong will that I, unfortunately, landed in jail for a few hours. I remember how upset I felt due to this ordeal, and after the court exonerated me, I remember thinking of blaming the policemen who arrested me and making them pay. Although I did not see this through, the thought lingered on my mind for a very long time. The point of this preamble is to tell you that doing time in prison evokes some malicious thoughts in the heart of a man. Even worse, when you are arrested for a crime that you didn't commit.

Nelson Mandela was incarcerated for 27 years for treason – a crime so vague, they just needed an excuse to put him behind bars. He went in with dark hair, and by the time he was released, his hair was grey. He was separated from family, friends, and the comfort of his home for 27 years. By the time he was out, some of his children had already started families of their own. Twenty-seven years behind bars is a long time for a man to come out and not be spiteful. Nelson Mandela's will to forgive is one of his most enviable character traits. Mandela knew that what was best for his people was racial harmony. That meant forgiving without forgetting and sharing power. *"We have to surprise [the white minority] with restraints and generosity,"* he said. A master of symbolism, Mandela invited his prison guards to the presidential swearing-in ceremony.

- **A Desire to Serve:** Many ask why we celebrate Mandela the way we do when he did nothing for Nigeria. Some say why only him, when so many others fought and died in the same battle for freedom. Others point out that we idolize him like a god when he was just as flawed as the next man. The man in question would be among this last set of people as he clearly said in an interview, *"My first task when I came out was to destroy that myth that I was something other than an ordinary human being."* I do not deny his humanity; instead, I am inspired by it: the living proof that man can, ultimately, be a leader who puts the need and interest of those he leads first. This is one of the many reasons why Mandela remains a celebrated hero.

- **The Willingness to Hand Over Power:** After being elected South Africa's first black president, Mandela announced he would serve only one term, though two were permissible. Mandela did not attempt to have the constitution amended to remove the two-term limit; a move that many might have supported wholeheartedly; instead, he only had the intention of serving one term, which he did, and left office June 14, 1999, "with nothing": no looting, no greed for power, no hidden agenda. He simply understood that rallying the country and bridging diverse interests meant making room for others. The philosopher Lao Tzu said the following: *"A leader is best when people barely know he exists, when his work is done, his aim fulfilled, they will say: we did it ourselves."* We are burdened with too many leaders wanting and demanding accolades they believe they deserve; even worse, when they don't deserve it.

Nelson Mandela, whether talking about his fight against apartheid, his time in prison, his emergence as a global icon, or speaking about anything, his words often have a resonance far beyond their original context. He exhibited an uncanny wisdom most cannot comprehend, and his perspective on leadership remains unequalled; one of his values as a leader is found in his words, *"It is better to lead from behind and to put others in front, especially when you celebrate victory when nice things occur. You take the front line when there is danger. Then people will appreciate your leadership."*

No leader has inspired anything like the devotion and reverence that Mandela did, and Africa cries out for great leaders like him. For our leaders have shown there is precious little to admire and much more to lament. Indeed, it doesn't seem far-fetched to call Mandela the last of the great ones; a truly inspirational historical leader in his own class. Who will pick up his mantle? We can only hope and strive to seek out one. Thus, the call is made, and the race is set: Will any step up?

The Young Shall Grow

Leaders who fail to provide authentic and proper governance, direction and strategic vision for the people leave a battered nation, as they continue to delude themselves and mislead the people within a losing legacy. The failures of the present-day leadership and the near collapse of our leadership structure makes it clear that not only has the leadership failed, but the followership has also failed.

Therefore, there is a need to begin a serious conversation on how to remedy the situation before we become unable to govern and be ungovernable. With all these in mind, I have chosen to borrow the operational name from the popular transport company that commutes major routes in the country, "The Young Shall Grow," as the title for this piece.

In the good old days, we had a culture of succession,

where the baton was passed from the older generation to the younger to carry on the legacy. A culture that leaders, especially in commerce, were developed in, unlike what we seem to have today where the young are not prepared to walk through succession to leadership positions and the old not ready to relinquish control of these leadership positions. I have always been committed to succession, as that is the real test of any leader. Leaving behind a path that others can tread and go further than you could ever go is the real definition of success.

With this realization, following the awareness my three expeditions created in the area of climate change and the environment, I decided that my fourth expedition would be different. My team and I developed it into a reality TV show called "Desert Warrior" where 44 men and women would cross the desert with me into Agadez, Niger Republic. The show was mainly to test young men and women interested in making a difference in the environment by subjecting them to exercises that will test their endurance and prepare them for the challenging leadership world that we all face today.

Before the fourth expedition, the third also ensured youth participation was at the forefront of it. The actions of the Lagos State Government at this time on greening the city and raising environmental awareness coincided with plans for my third expedition, which was in full swing. Governor Fashola sent his representative, Dr. Muiz Banire, the Honourable Commissioner for the Environment to the flag-off of the Desert Warriors. The third expedition involved seven young men and women driving from Lagos through the Sahara Desert to London.

Therefore, with the success of the third expedition and the impact it had on the youth in educating them about the dangers of desert encroachment and degradation of our green life, we decided to create a reality show to propagate the campaign further.

The Desert Warrior reality TV show in Agadez was a desert boot camp; an environmental protection task-based television show designed to educate and inform the viewing audience, as well as participants on the dangers of climate change, desertification and illegal migration from the north. The journey started on February 2, 2010. We were flagged off by Governor Fashola who was accompanied by the Commissioner for Environment, Dr. Muiz Banare and Dr. Titi Anibaba, the Permanent Secretary in the Ministry. There were 44 contestants in total, 18 support staff (media personnel, medical staff, officials from the Ministry of Environment) and five FADE officials.

The contestants on the reality show were very hands-on and showed much determination. They vigorously pursued their daily tasks which included, early morning fitness training, search and find assignments, car handling skills and Man O' War activities. Some of these tasks proved very demanding for the contestants, and others were downright dangerous and had to be scrapped or modified. In addition to these competitive tasks, the contestants were also engaged in some community services. Some of the tasks include tree planting, land reclamation and animal husbandry.

The Desert Warrior reality show was a huge success. Following the success of the reality show, we considered making it a yearly event, but due to the insurgencies that erupted across Africa around the period, we had to put a stop to it. Still, many of the young people who participated in the show have gone ahead to begin their own initiatives, and some pursue a career in the environment. However, the same cannot be said of everyone as some only participated for the thrill and adventure, which isn't bad in itself but does nothing to advance the cause.

Many young people I speak with today are interested in becoming entrepreneurs someday and hiring staff to work for them, yet some of this same group of young men and women are not willing to work for anyone or just downright act very lackadaisical at their place of employment. Some of these young ones tend to forget that before the student becomes the master, the student must go through various phases of training to sharpen his skills and prepare him for the position of leadership. How can you teach if you haven't learnt? How can you walk if you haven't crawled?

The young shall indeed grow. I hope that the young become unapologetic about developing an insatiable thirst for knowledge and determined to be a disciplined student through the process of growth. The young must begin by taking a leaf from the recent writing by Bashorun J.K Randle and his concern for the Nigerian project. He believed that the present generation of leaders has misdirected the population due to severe head injuries. The young must, therefore, bring out their brains, have it examined, and if needed, cured of the head injuries inflicted by years of misrule and bad examples.

Much Ado About Power - I

Electrical power demand in many African countries is likely to grow at more than six percent per annum over the next few decades, but even worse for hugely populated countries like Nigeria, compared to little over one percent in the developed world. This will require huge capital investments which may not be available then if the power sectors in these countries continue to perform as badly as they do now. It also has serious environmental implications for the countries themselves and the world at large, as people find other unfriendly means to generate their own power. Steps can be taken now to reduce both capital needs and environmental impacts by more than one half if the operational performance of the power sectors in these countries could be improved and brought up to standards prevailing in the developed world.

For over five decades, electrical power has been to this country like a mirage, and the poor power situation has been a hot topic on our lips. Thus, I will be discussing the damage, the fracture, the injury and the near collapse of our nation over the issue of power or the lack of it. Some time ago, I stumbled across the news in a national newspaper that the total electricity generation in the country has remained below 4,000 megawatts in the past few decades. Even more mind-boggling is the fact that despite the inadequate megawatts being generated, consumption is even much lower because we lack the capacity for efficient distribution.

Many countries of lesser resources have been able to provide constant electricity to their citizens as against the politics of shame that we have. Any President or leader of this great nation, Nigeria, that is able to give affordable electricity known as power to every Nigerian will be asked by almost 200 million Nigerians to remain President or leader for Life! Although this could not happen without amending the constitution as the will of the people alone cannot override the constitution.

In discussing power generation in Nigeria, I can go back as far as Murtala Mohammed and Olusegun Obasanjo era of the mid to late 70s; then power generation was the priority of those governments outside fighting corruption. An act of Parliament established ECN (Electricity Corporation of Nigeria) in 1951 with the singular role of powering the nation. In 1962, the Niger Dams Authority (NDA) was also established for the development of Hydro-Electric Power. However, a merger of the two was made in 1972 to form the National Electric Power Authority (NEPA), which as a result of unbundling and the power reform process, was renamed Power Holding Company of Nigeria (PHCN). From that regime to date, nobody has been able to tell Nigerians the amount of money we have spent trying to solve this power problem. We currently generate below 7000MW for 200 million Nigerians over a period of 40 years. Even by changing the name of the corporation severally, as mentioned above - which is the Nigerian thing to do when a body or organization is failing, as there is this superstition that when you change the name it will bring a new direction – we are yet to see any difference.

Between Buhari and Obasanjo as Heads of State, and Obasanjo and Buhari as Presidents, we have generated 6000MW then down to 3000MW then up to 7000MW without a proper explanation to the people for the rocky movement of power generation. How is it possible that billions of dollars, most of the amount borrowed from international funding agencies, go down the drain without anyone being held accountable and we the people have not demanded it?

The fight against corruption cannot be won in darkness because light everywhere will take people away from poverty, and once again, Nigeria will become a member of the League of Nations.

Nigerians have become so passive, and if we continue this way, more billions will go through us or past us without the power that we so much desire. It is important to note that when money is borrowed from both international and local funding agencies, they usually protect their loan by hiring consultants who handle repayments of the loan and oversee whatever the loan was meant for. Why is it in Nigeria that these funding agencies seem to either abandon or not bother protecting their loans, leaving us to opt for debt relief and debt forgiveness frequently?

In these 40 years of epileptic power supply to our nation, I can tell you of a few setbacks that have befallen the nation because of the power situation. Many genuine and reputable investors will not come to Nigeria because they see the few remaining multinationals struggling, with some of them having to replace four to five giant generators every few years. There are also many multinationals coming from countries which have signed onto the Paris Climate Change Protocol and see the generator issue as unsustainable because they know the damage these generators do to the environment and general health of the people as a result of air pollution. The health implications, the breathing problem, the eyesight and the hearing, especially for those above fifty contribute to the short life span expectancy we have in this country. The few striving institutions like telecommunications, financial bodies and the oil and gas sector pay huge taxes to the federal government coffers every year. All of them will rather pay double the tax burden if they did not have to buy generators and fuel ever so often. Hundreds of schools in Nigeria function with generators and spend so much on fuel, pushing the cost of a good education beyond the reach of the low and middle class. The same goes for all the hospitals, which has affected the way we address our healthcare. I can only begin to imagine the waste that has become cancer in the body of this nation and may kill us if nothing is done quickly. Here, the only winners are the manufacturers of the generators, the importers of fuel and the powers that be in the country, as they do not wish for a change from the present situation.

With the problems of distribution of power and transmission of power, even the 7000MW claimed to be generated cannot be adequately supplied to the nation. The transmission system in Nigeria does not cover every part of the country. It currently has the capacity to transmit between 3000MW - 4000MW, and it is technically weak, thus, susceptible to major disturbances. Let's compare our situation with two other nations of varied population size and power generation output:

South Africa is a nation that has achieved constant power with a population of almost 60 million people, and they currently generate 100,000MW. Brazil, on the other hand, has a population of about 200 million, and they currently generate between 120,000MW - 130,000MW, and although they have achieved stable power in most areas, there are still certain areas that power outages are regular. With these examples, you can draw your own conclusion on what Nigeria needs to achieve constant power. However, Generation of power is one thing while Transmission of power is another. Even if we were able to generate 100,000MW, our present capacity for distribution could not adequately transmit it, so I think before we continue asking for an increase to Power generation, we look into the ability to transmit that power adequately.

We, as a people, must begin to ask, "when will power change in Nigeria?" Could the reason for our epileptic power supply and other problems Nigeria faces be because the same people have been allowed to stay at the helm of political power for the past 40 years?

Much Ado About Power - II

In the first part of *"Much Ado About Power"*, we focused on the over 50 years of epileptic power supply Nigeria has endured, mostly due to a lack of effective leadership. I opined that the fight against corruption could not be won in darkness because light everywhere will take people away from poverty and enable Nigeria to become, once again, a member of the League of Nations.

However, this second part will be about a different kind of power. Taking from my book, *Hunger For Power,* I refer to power as a whole multitude of things, from influence to ambition to change. When people hear 'power' they think immediately of position or an office, but power is a range of different things. Power is many things to many people. It is like fire. On one hand, it can give you light while on the other hand, it can burn you. It can cook you a meal to perfection or it can raze your house completely leaving only ashes behind. It can purify gold and can just as easily calcify a human being.

Importantly, what fascinates me about power is what it does, its ability to change lives, influence outcomes, and sometimes destroy destinies. That fascination is what birthed my book and inspired the writing of this part: a deep desire to make sense of power and gain a little insight into the origins, workings and impact of power on men and women, and people and nations.

I remember an advert I saw many years ago for Pirelli Tyres. It was a simple Ad, but it packed a punch. It said simply: ***Power Is Nothing without Control.*** That Ad, which featured legendary Olympian, Carl Lewis, made it to the front pages of newspapers across the globe, won many awards, and was even included in a book – "The 100 Best Posters of the Century." It was, to put mildly, a powerful Advert.

In ancient Greece, fire was regarded as the most potent symbol of power, and that was why when Prometheus approached Zeus and asked to be allowed to take fire to the people Zeus refused. Consumed by his belief that fire would make men happier and change the course of their lives, Prometheus stole fire from Mount Olympus and gave it to men. Then he paid dearly for his action.

This has been the lot of many men for centuries. Men, who were hankering after power, sought it with all the resources at their disposal only to destroy lives and careers along the way in their mad quest for power. Think about them; Genghis Khan, Napoleon Bonaparte, Adolf Hitler, Idi Amin Dada, Saddam Hussein, Muamar Ghaddafi, and many others still living, even in our country, Nigeria. They sought power, they obtained it, and it destroyed them but unfortunately, not just them alone.

The most humbling contemporary tale of power sought, obtained and handled deftly must be that of Nelson Mandela. Mandela, not a saint by any stretch of the imagination, fought for his people's freedom, spent 27 years in jail, was released and then elected the first president of newly independent South Africa. But then after just one term in office, a man who spent 27 years in jail waiting for the very thing he had obtained, stepped down from power and handed over without rancour. His selflessness and exemplary leadership have been hailed world over, but what continues to interest and intrigue me is his lack of avarice; that consuming hunger for power – to obtain it, to wield it and not to let go of it.

I will like to explain the similarities in the power I discussed in Part 1, electrical power, and the one I refer to here, political power. Both have the intensity to create change, to better lives and to solve problems if supplied in the right amount and through the appropriate channel; however, the real essence of both seem to be lacking in my country.

One of the most important functions of any modern government is to keep the power flowing. Electrical power is the driver of modern society, keeping industry functioning effectively hospitals working efficiently 24/7, streetlights lit, water flowing, elevators riding, and computers, air conditioners, and refrigerators humming. In most modern societies, the government runs, manages or regulates the power grid. That means that any failure, disruption or collapse of that grid reasonably falls on government leaders; the people hold the leaders accountable.

Let me share an incident that depicts a clear example of the reality of leadership and power. In 2003, there were a series of power blackouts in California, USA, caused by market manipulations and capped retail electricity prices. It affected all aspects of the state - businesses and homes, and the citizens didn't take that too well, so they exercised their right as a people, to hold accountable, the leaders that they voted into power to serve them; this led to the recall of a sitting governor, Gray Davis, and a special election held for his replacement, Arnold Schwarzenegger. The power of the people was in full control, overriding the power of the leader. The economic fall-out of the lack of electrical power significantly harmed the sitting governor.

Around the world, governments owe citizens to deliver electricity to them or face voter wrath. Electrical power that is reliable and predictable is an economic necessity and the key to giving government and leaders legitimacy. In proper democratic societies, "no electrical power" means "reduced or no political power" for governing parties and a ripe opportunity for opposition movements. But in Nigeria, the reverse appears to be the case: "No electrical power" means, not only "greater political power", but also richer pockets for the leaders.

Nigeria is a country where our leaders see their positions of power as a way to make their lives better and not a responsibility to work for those that bestow the power on them. You may wonder, why then, in a democracy, have the people allowed this ugly power play? The simple answer is that many decades of the frequent barrage of coups, corrupt leadership and bad policies have caused economic and political crises, creating an easy pathway to power for anyone with a "cheap promise" of a better economy. Post-independence, Nigeria's circumstances changed for the continuously worse, causing the people to lose faith and trust in the system. Now, when people finally lose faith in a system, more often than not, they also lose all sense of belonging - patriotism; they cease to care about the system, and simply focus on self. Thus, with patriotism lost, power then becomes exposed to be stolen, and someone who would never attract a crowd in normal circumstances would rise to steal and bestow power upon himself.

As citizens of Nigeria, we have the real power to decide who gets to lead us, but for too long we have left this power in the hands of a select few because we gave up too soon. So, the question is, how long are "we the people" going to continue to allow power to be stolen from us? When are "we the people" going to take our rightful place as "king makers" and bestow power on a worthy leader?

PART V

THE HERDSMEN SAGA

"Critical to the fight against global terrorism is an ability to move beyond presuppositions and stereotypes in our attitudes and policies and to form partnerships that transcend an 'us' and 'them' view of the world."

— John L. Esposito

Discovering the Desert and Herdsmen

I have driven, lived and studied the desert for over 40 years. My expedition across the Sahara Desert started in the 60s, driving from London to Lagos, and back after some years. However, this second time around, I had a theme; I had seen too much devastation on my first trip and subsequent studies to continue to keep quiet. The theme was "Global warming is Climate Change and Climate Change is Desertification, Drought and Famine."

After the second expedition, I have returned to the desert two more times; a total of four times and written several books about it. It is noteworthy to know that the second book I published titled, *Me, My Desert and I,* in 2002 was dedicated to the stateless and homeless people of the desert who have lost their land and boundaries to the Sahara, and other deserts of the world. This shows that the signs have always been there, but only a few of us paid attention to it. This was the start of my environmental non-profit organisation, Fight Against Dessert Encroachment (FADE Africa).

My third book, "Bridging the Sahara" came after various studies on the science of desertification at the Ben Gurion University, Israel, in 2002 and sojourn to other deserts of the world such as China, Arizona and Nevada. It proffered solutions to the encroaching desert and land degradation that was preemptive and sustainable. During my stint in the desert, I encountered thousands of herdsmen, numerous cattle, and I got used to their culture, way of life and way of travelling. It became apparent in my subsequent desert sojourns just how much the disappearing greenery affected the herdsmen.

• The Disappearing Greenery: Cause and Effect

In the early 70s and 80s, the catastrophic Sahelian droughts engulfed the entire Sahel region of Africa with a punishing period of low to absent rainfall, poor harvest and extended famine that lasted for years. The countries that suffered most are Nigeria,

Niger, Sudan, and Ethiopia. Farmlands were lost to dust from the Sahara and people watched their farms and investments in animal husbandry disappear in a matter of months. These droughts devastated the greenery and the grass covers that provided grazing fields for the livestock in Northern Nigeria. For centuries, the nomadic Fulani had adopted historical shifting culture in their farming practices. The shepherds will move their animals from grazing fields to grazing fields while depleted fields are left to be nurtured to life by the rains. Now and again, they would gather a few hundred animals, drive them through urban centres for sales at certain markets along their routes, grazing them along the way, travelling by foot, sometimes all the way to Lagos. Some of them come as far away as Chad, Niger, Senegal, and Mauritania. After the sales, they would return to their farms in the North, and others to their countries. Unfortunately, these droughts of the 70s and 80s laid their farms and grazing fields to wastelands, while the advancing Sahara that deposited dust over the fields turned them into arid lands.

It was clear that if left unchecked, the disappearance of these grazing fields and greenery would create desperation that would only result in chaos. This we can see today.

• Mitigating Actions by Government

Over the years, the Federal Government has embarked on programmes and initiatives to stem the advancing Sahara. We at FADE have collaborated with the Federal Government on some of these programmes. Our position paper on drought and desertification was part of what led to the creation of the Ministry of Environment, the then "Shelter Belt commission" which never saw the light of day and now the "Great Green Wall" project. The programmes established by these initiatives and bodies mostly tend to address tree planting as measures to slow down or combat desertification in the Sahelian regions. Despite these efforts and those of about 11 different agencies and departments within the Federal Government charged with the restoration of greenery in the northern states, no concerted effort had been devoted to the restoration or creation of grazing fields. The attitudinal approach of the state governments, which have jurisdiction over these lands, and the farmers have tended towards neglect. The result is that despite the huge sums of money voted, there exist virtually no grazing fields in the north, even around the river basin authorities, to cater for the rising population of animals currently being farmed to feed Nigeria's growing population.

Today, there are talks and efforts within the National Assembly to establish grazing fields across the country. This is an over-reach, as you do not need the force of the law to regenerate lost farmlands. What is needed is the empowerment of all these bodies to carry out their mandate to the letter.

• Shepherds Turn Marauders

Herein lies the crux of the matter. It appears we have many armies without a division, and we don't know where most of these armies are coming from or what they are fighting for. It is important to note that the herdsmen I saw in the past were not armed. All they had was their knives, though poisonous, to wade off dangerous animals. The questions we should be asking are: Where are they getting these arms? Who is training and funding them?

It is an irony of facts that within the abhorrent rhetoric lies some fundamental truths. The so-called clash between farmers and herdsmen is not merely a clash; it is an attack on businesses and human lives. It is good to remember that the farmers are engaged in their own private business, farming within their own real estate. The herdsmen are also engaged in their own private business of animal husbandry, but in another man's real estate, having been forced to abandon their own lands by desertification.

It is important to note that these occupants have shown no respect to their host communities; they have shown no regards to the customs of the people or their sacred lands, nor their farmlands. These same shepherds do not walk their animals through their own farms in their lands. But here in the Middle Belt and the South, they do not have any compulsion in letting these animals trample and feed on vegetable farms and other crops with reckless abandon. This is deliberate and unacceptable, and so is their occupation. Such attitudes lead to conflicts. To refuse to recognise these facts is disingenuous, unjust, and being in denial.

Summarily, the wanton destruction of lives and property has been the bane of the Nigerian culture since the amalgamation. And the consistent choice of the authorities to look the other way only serves to embolden the next militia. This is not leadership when you do not hold people accountable for their actions and atrocities.

This phenomenon, in conjunction with mediocrity, accounts for the failures of all reforestation and desert combating programmes initiated in the country since the 1960s; this will only spell doom for the nation.

It then appears that the president seems to be abandoning his bottom-up approach to addressing Nigeria ills, which was the hallmark of his military leadership. Considering his division of power constraint, he has not been in touch with the people as was expected.

Indeed, there have been talks of war, impending or imagined. But I will caution, let us not talk about war because if it happens, there will be nothing left of Nigeria. If war occurs, there will be no flow of oil; the farmers cannot produce, leading to food scarcity and starvation. The country may disintegrate into anarchy, which is worse than war because you may not know who your enemy is or where to find him, as over a third of our population has no address. Few people will most certainly make money from such a war, and a few others will leave the country. But the majority will stay back and suffer.

The Untamed Sahara: The Origin of The Herdsmen Crisis

History tells us that the Sahara once had a very different environment. We are told that the drylands showed signs of pastoralism, large settlements, herding and pottery in Libya and Algeria, dating back to 7000BC. For centuries, trans-Saharan traders voyaged in both directions between the Mediterranean countries and the countries of sub-Saharan Africa. Economies were being formed, and people made a living until the effects of desertification and global warming changed everything.

Now, those changes brought on by desertification and global warming have destroyed lives and properties in many regions. It becomes paramount to clearly state again at this point something I have campaigned for over the past six decades that the development and security of the continent of Africa will continue to suffer until the Sahara which is the biggest desert in the word is tamed.

In the 60s, when the Sahara occupied only about a fifth of the land area of Africa, President Kwame Nkrumah of Ghana made the famous declaration that the continent of Africa will remain in darkness until the trans-Saharan highway is built. This never happened, and today, the desert has expanded and occupies over a third of the land area of Africa.

It is interesting to note that Africa is the only continent in the world where you cannot move goods and services by road or by train from South to North or from East to West because of the Sahara. Our counterparts made the move to tame their deserts since the early 60s, leaving us behind in the advancement of civilization.

A good example is the Negev Desert that was not only tamed, but the whole of Israel was recovered from it. The father of Israel at that time, Ben Gurion, started by moving scientists to the desert and lived in the desert with the scientists while taming the desert. Eventually, Ben Gurion University was built there in the desert. Ben Gurion later went on to become the Prime Minister of Israel.

In the USA, the Nevada and Arizona deserts gave birth to Las Vegas. Taming these deserts were done to prevent the deserts not only from merging but from expanding. Las Vegas now boasts of a developed, thriving and modern city free from the woes of desertification.

In China, the Gobi Desert was the second largest to the Sahara. Today, not only has it been tamed; railways, roads and communities have been built through and in this desert. Massive agricultural developments have taken place in the Gobi Desert, and the population of the territory has grown from a few thousand to a few million in the last 40 years. The Chinese Academy of Science, where I did my study tour in 2002, is responsible for such a tremendous transformation of the Gobi Desert.

With many African countries becoming independent from their colonial masters, it was desirous to continue the age-old trade between the emerging economies. It was realized that with the industrial revolution, faster and bigger trading could be achieved if a road or rail link is established between the Mediterranean countries and the rest of Africa. So, following the statement by Kwame Nkrumah in 1964, African Heads of State under the hospices of the Organization of African Unity (now known as the African Union) started preliminary discussions that will lead towards establishing a structure for taming and bridging the Sahara.

Thus, was born the Trans-Saharan highway, a transnational highway project to pave, improve and ease border formalities on an existing trade route across the Sahara Desert. It runs between North Africa bordered by the Mediterranean Sea in the north and West Africa bordered by the Atlantic Ocean in the south; from Algiers in Algeria to Lagos in Nigeria.

Unfortunately, the Heads of State that originated the desert taming project were not able to see this plan to completion due to the various successful coup attempts on almost all their lives while in office. Although many experts say irrespective of the coups, the project was already doomed to fail due to poor planning. The era of the military cast a dark cloud on the structure established by the former Heads of State because bridging the Sahara was not a priority for the new military leaders.

As the end of the military era was drawing to a close, the climate debate started. It was at this point that many interested organizations like Fight Against Desert Encroachment (FADE) joined the discussion. We were in attendance at the first climate change convention in Brazil and also at subsequent conventions that recognized the effect global warming was having on the desert and the rest of our environment. That was what inspired the theme of my second expedition into the desert, which was *"Desertification is global warming and global warming is climate change."*

When the convention to combat desertification was inaugurated, FADE made a representation at the convention and was subsequently accredited by the convention. Those were exciting times; we all looked forward to a bright future that will right the wrongs of the past due to the course we were setting in the present. Unfortunately, for Africa, that bright future hasn't come as expected.

During my second expedition, I found out that most of the countries bordering the Sahara were looking up to Nigeria to take a leadership role in the fight against desertification. External Affairs ensured that our Nigerian Ambassadors received me in those countries, and the Ambassadors ensured that I interacted with the major stakeholders at press conferences. This was when I realised that they looked up to Nigeria for directions. They looked up to Nigeria because it was in Lagos, in 1964, that the protocol was first established. There is also the fact that we had the resources, both human and natural resources that will lead to the execution of such a monumental project.

It is difficult to understand why bridging the Sahara isn't at the forefront of many African nations' development plans, especially Nigeria. We are already experiencing the effects of not taming the Sahara from the herder-farmer clashes to the frequent deaths of our countrymen making illegal journeys across the desert to Europe. Following FADE's accreditation by UNEP (United Nations Environmental Program), we realised the magnitude of the whole project of bridging the Sahara and approached well-disciplined professional bodies like the Nigerian Society of Engineers (NSE) and Federation of African Engineers (FAE) to pioneer and take this agenda to perpetuity. Although the project has not taken off as planned, the potential was enormous. A bridged Sahara, and by this, I mean developing a proper road network in the desert, will open up the desert to enable the smooth movement of goods, trade, and services across the continent. It will create employment, education, and industry for millions of Africans that border the Sahara through many countries. It will also green a good part of the Sahara and provide grazing fields for the development of animal husbandry.

Cultural practices in Africa make people congregate around places with good roads, agricultural lands, water, and perhaps, electricity. If the road networks are built and maintained, people will move around in search of trades. When they do, they will stop around in places for a brief stay which will attract others willing to provide certain services that may be required. That is the process in which settlements and communities are created.

Migration will reduce significantly as it will make monitoring of the desert a lot easier for countries. Countries could set up a joint task force that will guard the Sahara. This will go a long way in stemming conflict or wars and the security risk that follows.

To further improve life, vegetative cover will be required. This will protect the roads from the severe effects of the desert sand storms. With the vegetation in the desert, there will be a change in rainfall patterns. Simply put, the rains will begin to fall in the desert with the greening of the land once again. There will also be a need to supply water for the different projects which will lead to the availability of potable water to millions of people in the Sahel.

Finally, the greening will stop the encroachment, especially if done right with the necessary land reclamation techniques employed. An obvious benefit is the recovery of lands that have been encroached upon by the untamed desert for agricultural and grazing purposes. This will also help boost countries' economies as farmers that may have migrated due to loss of the fertile lands will return with hopes of experiencing higher yields. Inevitably, the threat to food security will be minimized, and poverty will be reduced.

Paying lip service to combat environmental degradation by our governments will only further destroy our fertile lands. What is required now is action, albeit one that has taken a long time to come. Like the popular ancient native American quotes says, *"we do not inherit the earth from our ancestors, we borrow it from our children."* The admonition is that we leave behind a world for which our children will not curse us.

Beyond the Herders-Farmers crisis

Nigeria has been grappling with varied security challenges, chief among them in recent times is the herders-farmers crisis. Underpinning the escalation of this crisis is a confluence of environmental and demographic forces. With this confluence, comes a rapid depletion of arable land for subsistence farming, especially along the Lake Chad basin, which in turn, ignited the violent clashes between herdsmen and farmers. Thus, the surface treatment that is being given to the crisis is unacceptable, as these violent clashes over grazing lands between local farmers and pastoral herdsmen has resulted in the daily loss of human lives, the destruction of people's livelihood, and the serious threat to the security of the nation. The nation is at this stage of the crossroad because we are not prepared to accept our past mistakes and the neglect we have subjected our land to; neglect that is causing the land to fight back.

For many years, we watched Lake Chad receding, and we did nothing to check it. We built over six river basin authorities for the supply of potable drinking water and irrigation. The irrigation was also to promote two seasonal cropping in the year, which would bring about food security in most of the dry land regions that have lost their capacity. However, that didn't happen. Thus, the communities that were to settle around the Chad and river basin authorities were left stranded.

In the 80s and 90s, after the great drought, almost all the states in Nigeria, including the Federal Capital Territory, Abuja, embarked on ceremonial tree planting campaigns. If the trees had survived, most of Nigeria would now be a big forest; instead, Nigeria lost over 35 percent of its forest cover between the 60s and 2000.

Nigeria had tried various strategies in the past at tackling desertification and the effect it has on rural development, but these failed to achieve much because of various political, economic, and social characteristics of the Nigerian population. Instead, we watched as the advancing Sahara brought desertification and rendered arable lands infertile, causing all the greenery and grazing fields to disappear.

My various journeys across the Sahara vividly portrayed the deteriorating conditions of the people of the desert and the continuing consequences of desertification. I have seen how towns and communities dwindle in size, and in some cases, disappear altogether. I have seen people migrate away from their communities heading south in search of better living conditions, leaving their homes to the advancing desert sand.

In over 40 years of my exploration of the Sahara, I have seen it grow in size. What we need to remember is that it has not always been like this. History tells us that the Sahara once had a very different environment. Researchers report that the Sahara shows signs of ancient rivers and traces of plants and animals deep beneath its sands - evidence of the plain's greener past. However, crop farmers grew diverse species of plants that left the Saharan soil exposed. They also brought livestock that ate the vegetation without replenishment, further uncovering the soil, much like what is happening in the northern region of the country currently. The implication of grazing the greenery without replenishment is that the land becomes vulnerable to the encroachment of the Sahara, giving rise to migration.

Historically, the Fulani herdsmen are nomadic and habitually migratory, moving annually from

North to South in search of grazing fields and markets for their herds. However, the movement which used to be seasonal has been altered due to expansive desertification, drought and gully erosion in Northern Nigeria. The herdsmen now seek greener pasture southward, wreaking havoc as they devour crops and forcefully appropriate lands.

• Migration and Proper Documentation

It is essential to recognise that many of these herdsmen are not all our countrymen. I am aware that the movements of shepherds begin as far as from Mauritania, Mali, Chad, Niger, and Cameroon. It is imperative to document the migration to ascertain the particular country they are coming from and the number of animal heads that they are bringing into Nigeria. Without relinquishing the "big brother" role we play in Ecowas and the rest of the continent, we need to realise that we cannot keep welcoming foreigners without proper documentation. This is dangerous and might be damaging to the security of Nigeria.

Secondly, if we must continue to allow the inflow of our nomadic shepherds from outside Nigeria, then we must establish movement corridors for them to follow without stampeding on people's farmland, or better still, have the animals muzzled when passing through farmland like it is done in other parts of the world.

It is vital to emphasize on the fact that the herdsmen are engaged in the private business of animal husbandry, just like the farmers are engaged in their own private business. We must not allow one business to destroy the other.

The recent announcement by the Inspector General of Police about steps being taken to begin the immediate disarming of the herdsmen is a welcome development and much in line with the short-term measures to be considered. I recall in the 80s when I wanted to purchase a gun. I had to apply for a license to own and handle one. The then Inspector General of Police, Jimeta Gambo, met with me and insisted on first consulting with my wife before approving for me to be issued a license. He also strongly advised that I go for a course to learn how to handle the weapon. Only then, was I issued the license to purchase a gun. Afterwards, I was required to register the weapon with the authorities. This is far from the case today, another pointer at the failure of our system.

We need to realise that there are those working

to destabilise Nigeria for varied reasons; many of whom will profit hugely from a fractured nation. These people have an army of their own and have been fighting the Nigerian army for years. These "armies" are now recruiting mercenaries who used to be part of defeated militias such as in Libya, Isis, and Boko haram. These mercenaries can be seen masquerading amongst the shepherds.

• Medium To Long-Term Measures

Disarming the herdsmen and regulating their movement across the nation will only cover the wound in the short term. It will not heal it. The only way to effectively tackle the intensified migration of herdsmen is to return greenery to those states devastated by desertification, gully erosion, and drought.

The first milestone to aim for should be the establishment of grazing fields in the impacted states. To do this, we must also create water bodies by these locations both to nurture the grazing fields and for consumption by the animals. The investment costs can be borne by the government fully at this stage. However, the owners of the animals who graze there shall be made to pay for feeding and watering their animals.

While these water bodies and green fields are being established, trees should be planted to serve as windbreakers on the windward sides to push back sand dunes accumulation. If well managed, in four years, the grazing fields will mature.

The long-term plan involves the establishment of ranches by the animal owners in the same way the government has established the grazing fields. It is the responsibility of the farmers to pen their animals. Domestic animals are not supposed to be free rangers. Meat production is a private business that should be governed by applicable laws and statutes of the States and the Federal Government.

Conclusively, I reiterate, war is not an option, and can never be an option; all well-meaning nationalists and peace-loving Nigerians should discountenance war. However, to ensure that peace reigns, we must start now to make amends. We must commit ourselves to begin again and sustain the process of returning the Lake Chad to its original position. This is not rocket science but will require us to turn away from business as usual. There will also be the need to refurbish the river basin authorities to its original capacity and open up the number of irrigation canals that were created to supply water to the farmlands.

We need to understand that a southward migration

for grazing will only further make the encroachment of the Sahara easier, especially if we do not replenish what we have taken from the land.

Anti-Grazing Or Open Grazing Laws: Not The Solution

As already established, several years ago, climate change brought along with it, drought and desertification that ravaged all the settlements and hamlets along the fringes of the Sahara. The land of the nomadic people became dust as greenery and water bodies disappeared. At that time, millions of Africans, particularly the nomadic Fulanis that stretches all the way to Mauritania, started to move in search of greener pastures. Sadly, drought and desertification led to the death of millions of animal heads.

The devastating effect of climate change on land is evident. There are sufficient facts to this:

There's the fact that climate change resulted in the vulnerability of the natural shelter belt along the

Benue-Plateau Corridor. Another fact is that the people of Benue-Plateau accommodated the migration at the initial stage but started to object when the migration not only became permanent, but the number went from thousands to millions.

Then due to uncontrolled grazing, the land of the people of Benue became a savannah. The attempts by the people and government of these states to resist the overgrazing activities led to the increase in crisis and confusion.

Benue-Plateau State was a former administrative division of Nigeria which existed as a single state until February 3rd, 1976 when it was divided into two states - Benue and Plateau. The city of Jos was the capital of Benue-Plateau State.

A good majority of farmers in these affected states also suffered and still suffer great loses due to changes in farming seasons and drylands. The losses gave rise to migration, leading to increased conflict which is why many of them are now in IDP camps.

An indisputable fact is that hundreds, and maybe, thousands of lives have been lost over the years.

Grazing activities have become a prevalent debate in our nation. Citizens are concerned about what policies the government is putting in place to curb the menace that has stemmed from open grazing activities in parts of the country.

The solution to this problem lies in well-articulated stage developments:

- **STAGE 1:** Government should consider imposing an immediate ceasefire to be brokered by a non-partisan body of three to four men and women that may not be Nigerians.

- **STAGE 2:** Tracing the origin of the migration of herders as far back as possible to determine the original abode of herders, particularly since some of them may have come from outside the country.

- **STAGE 3:** While steps 1 and 2 listed above are going on, work must commence immediately to re-establish the grazing fields along the fringes of the Sahara to reinstate and resettle the herders in their original habitats.

Soon after the crisis started, I wrote a piece in the Vanguard Newspapers titled, *Beyond the Herdsmen -Farmers Crisis.* The finding and the solutions I proffered were based on my research in the last 40 years traversing the Sahara, studying the effect of the drought, climate change, and land degradation as a result of desertification, and understanding the nomadic Fulani pattern of movement, migration, and pastoral business. In that piece, I wrote, and I quote *"In over 40 years of my exploration of the Sahara, I have seen it grow in size. What we need to remember is that it has not always been like this. History tells us that the Sahara once had a very different environment. Researchers report that the Sahara shows signs of ancient rivers and traces of plants and animals deep beneath its sands – evidence of the plain and greener past. However, crop farmers grew species of plants that left the Saharan soil exposed. They also brought livestock that ate the vegetation without replenishment, further uncovering the soil. Much like what is currently happening in the northern region of the country. The implication of grazing the greenery without replenishment makes the land vulnerable to the encroachment of the Sahara and the dust giving rise to migration."*

The two important businesses highlighted in my piece are very vital for the economic and cultural development of the country: the herders and their animal husbandry practice, and the farmers and their lands – both are the food basket of the nation. These two businesses contribute immensely to the national GDP and are amongst two of the largest employers of labour in the country.

They sustain the land, contribute to the poverty

alleviation program of the country and fostering harmony between neighbours. These two businesses must not crash, but instead, they should complement each other. However, their survival is dependent on the curtailing of the food and security crises being experienced at the moment.

As we move further into this discussion, we need to understand nomadic Fulani movement and their activities that extend all the way to Senegal, Burkina Faso, Libya, Northern part of Ghana, and the Cameroons.

Therefore, when the drought, as a result of climate change and desertification occurred in the late 70s and early 80s, most of the greenbelt and water bodies along the fringes of the Sahara got completely depleted, leaving the herders with very little grazing fields. It should be noted that long before now and for hundreds of years, the herders moved in accordance with climate change. Sometimes, they leave their lands for a few years so it can regain lost nutrients before they come back to it. This process of farming is known as shifting cultivation.

There was never any conflict, and the herders continued to move seasonally. It took them a few months to travel, and they got rid of the aged animals along the way, after which they returned to their hamlets.

As far as I can remember, during such journeys, they never trampled on anyone's farm and did not wish to be urbanized. Instead, they always returned home to their natural hamlets.

The biggest problem on our hands is that due to the porous borders between Nigeria, Cameroon, and Niger, with Nigeria being a buffer country with much greenery (especially in the middle belt), these countries' herders have joined their brothers in the North to invade parts of Nigeria.

Hundreds of nomads have entered the country with their thousands of animal heads. Those countries that were at war, such as Libya, Chad, migrated with their arms as the herders found them to be useful escorts. Now they have found a place in Nigeria, and this is very disturbing.

Coupled with the solutions that have already been proffered, it is crucial that we are having the right conversation and not once again politicising the situation at the detriment of human life.

PART I

THE ENVIRONMENT

"The Earth will not continue to offer its harvest, except with faithful stewardship. We cannot say we love the land and then take steps to destroy it for use by future generations."

— John Paul II

Climate Change: No Longer A Debate For The Distant Nations

In 2019, a United Nations expert cautioned that climate change "threatens to undo the last 50 years" of development, global health and poverty reduction. The UN Special Rapporteur on extreme poverty and human rights, Philip Alston, had said, *"Even if current targets are met, tens of millions will be impoverished, leading to widespread displacement and hunger."* He added that climate change could push more than 120 million more people into poverty by 2030 and will have the most severe impact in developing countries, regions, and the places poor people live and work.

It is worthy of note that the consequences of climate change include food insecurity, reduced crop yields, increased migration, and dramatic damage to coastal communities. Given this, I had previously written about the origins of the herdsmen crisis in Nigeria, and my focus then was to establish this link between the crisis and climate change. That wouldn't be my first time tackling the issue, and even proffering solutions in my media writings and interviews.

However, in line with the ECOWAS protocol on free movement which stipulates the right of ECOWAS citizens to enter, reside and establish economic activities in the territory of other member states, Nigeria, being the big brother of the continent, saw her population grow from 60 million people at independence to about 200 million people without proper documentation and statistics of how we got there.

It is nice to be able to harbour countries that have been affected by the phenomenon of climate change that brought about desertification, which in turn, damaged the grazing fields, greenery for farming, and water bodies throughout the fringes of the Sahara. It is also nice to be able to harbour migration from neighbouring countries, but we have to be mindful of the fact that if Nigeria should go down as a result of uncontrolled migration, many of these neighbouring countries will go down as well.

Permit me to digress slightly, but you see, the

open-door policy is not the problem. Unlike a certain world leader that seems adamant at building walls and changing laws to keep people away, I am pro-migration as I have benefitted greatly from the opportunity. My education benefitted from my ability to migrate. My adventures enabled me to mingle with people from different parts of the world that I crossed paths with and explored the many different cultures around us. So once again, I will like to clarify that migration is not the problem. It is inevitable. However, the problem is harbouring people from sub -regional countries without proper documentation which only makes nonsense of the ECOWAS free movement protocol. It is irresponsible of a nation not to make provisions for the security and overpopulation implications of migration, especially if the nation had been warned of the looming crisis. Climate change rang an early bell, but many chose to turn deaf ears to it.

I am aware that some of the shepherds who are very skilled in animal husbandry and have migrated from as far as Mauritania, Senegal, Niger, Chad and Northern Cameroons add some value to the economy so there's much that can be gained from this situation. However, bearing in mind that 11 states in Nigeria are equally affected by desertification at this point, I believe a necessary first step at addressing the problem will be a continental review of the protocol that has imposed this crisis on Nigeria.

Another urgent and most important step is to make investments in greening projects that will create new grazing fields in the homes and lands of these migrants to encourage them to go back to their countries.

I visited other deserts of the world before I proffered solutions to the encroachment of the Sahara. I visited the Gobi Desert in China, Nevada and Arizona deserts in the USA, and then I proceeded to the Ben Gurion University in Israel to study the Science of Desertification. All these countries tamed their desert and were able to prevent land degradation in the desert because they were able to put in place infrastructures that were preemptive and sustainable.

Importantly, we must understand that climate change simply means when the climate is overheated; it brings with it intense heatwave, bushfire, and turning the farmland into dust, thereby resulting in food scarcity. The overheating of the climate also leads to the torrential downpour of rain which brings about gully erosion. The sea level rises because of the warming, and when that happens, the low land Islands disappear, like the recent event in the Ayetoro region of Ondo state.

Most of the low land areas in Lagos that have settled below sea level because of the heavy developments that have taken place are very prone to the effects of climate change. Areas such as Victoria Island, the entire Lekki Peninsula, Banana Island, Parkview, and the fishing communities that settled along the coastal areas of the community, are under threat from heavy storms that generate waves which occur whenever the wind speed is more than 60km per hour.

Recently, the rains have been coming in relatively late, and when they do, they come very heavy and stormy. The situation is worse in some places, like in the case of Capetown, South Africa, where the town had gone for almost two years without rain. Capetown experienced one of the most severe cases of drought in over a century. They ran out of water, and all the dams also receded. Without normal rainfall, Capetown will continue to experience water shortages.

In some other cases, the rains are so heavy that it claims life and property due to flooding. In some parts of Nigeria, we are already experiencing flooding that has claimed lives and properties. There's also the significant danger in the rising sea level because the rivers and streams, which in Nigeria, are responsible for 80 percent of potable water receding. It can then be argued that if the change in climate continues, the sea water may contaminate the underground water resources. Many countries are afraid of this happening, and thus, are already introducing measures by building barrages. There's so much to learn from the mitigation and adaptation of infrastructure that are being put in place.

With the rise in global temperatures, it is my duty to tell what I know about the nomadic people of the continent. They are like one family. In the Middle East and Israel, they are known as Bedouins. They don't have boundaries and move across countries looking for grazing fields and water bodies; their culture and religion unite them, and they find home wherever they find greenery. In my local government area of Delta State, they have created a colony in a town that used to be known as Otulu, a small settlement of farmers from across the Niger. The population was only a few thousands a decade ago, but today, the population is over 10,000 and the original settlers are now the minority. It can be seen that climate change brought on with it the crisis of migration, and the security implication that we face is much more present, particularly in the middle belt and some parts of southern Nigeria, where the leaders and security agencies looked the other way when I predicted this crisis about 20 years ago.

Still on climate change, the most important festival of my people is the New Yam Festival. It is a cultural celebration that glorifies the hard work of the farmers and a period of reflection that prepares them for the next farming season. The idea is that the farmers plant in April, after the first big rain, and nurture the plants until the harvest in September. This ceremony is held annually in September and continues for about six weeks after the harvest of the yams. Now, the big rains don't come in April anymore but sometimes in May or early June. For that reason, the people can no longer have their harvest in September because it takes an average of five months from planting to harvesting. My people have remained resolute and have continued to have their ceremony without the yams or sometimes even importing the yams from other lands. I don't know how long their resolve will last, but it will be a pity to lose such an old tradition, thanks to the poor mitigation of climate change.

Climate change, therefore, is no longer a debate for the distant nations. It has affected the herdsmen, and their business of animal husbandry, and driven them away from their open space natural areas to urbanization which they never wanted. Climate change is also threatening the underground water resources and making them acidic. It is also causing the farming communities all over the country to change their farming calendar. That alone will bring about food security issues and serious threat to the security of the nation if this trend is allowed to continue.

Again, let it be understood that climate change is no longer a debate for the white man and the western world. Only fools will even still consider it a topic of debate. Climate change is our reality and only when we all come to realise this, can we begin to take the necessary steps to survive it. A pity we are still talking survival when other countries are thriving.

Fear For The Land: Managing Our Environment For A Sustainable Future

There is a common saying in my language by the elders that goes thus *"ndu ogonogo anidinma na ahudimma"* which when translated into English means "The journey to a long life and good health will depend on how well we protect and manage our environment".

Our forefathers did not cut down trees without replacing them. They did not graze the fields with their domestic animals without shifting or alternating grazing patterns. They did not also farm the lands without a shifting cultivation culture. Some of the foods they ate and some of the fruits they used for making soap, oil, and paint were nurtured from generations to generations. Some of these trees lived for hundreds of years. The mango trees, the orange trees and the cashew trees that I ate from when I was growing up are still there. The Neem trees, the Jatropha trees and the Rubber trees that gave us oil and rubber were planted all over the southern and northern parts of Nigeria. These trees have continued to produce. Those before us did not cut them down without replacing them. As a result, they did not have floods, and they did not have erosions. They did not have air pollution; their lands were filled with nutrients, and we could easily consume the food germinated without the aid of fertilizer.

It was also nice to know that a lot of the fruits and vegetables we ate came from birds and animals that migrated from other lands and brought with them fruits and seeds. All that gave us the biodiversity we have today. The sad news is that some of those animals no longer migrate to Nigeria due to climate change, and most of our forests have become savannahs and deserts. This is as a result of the disappearance of the vegetative covers that would normally absorb the rain, thereby resulting in the kinds of flooding we've seen in Delta, Kogi, Benue, Kano, Kaduna and Katsina.

That wasn't always the case as there was a time we never had to worry about desertification, we had rivers and water bodies running through the Sahara, and as such, the encroachment of the desert was contained. In the past few years, our waters and rivers have been badly polluted from oil spillages or bad waste management and disposal. Now and then, we hear the government will carry out some clean-up operations, maybe once every ten years, without involving the community and those who own the lands.

When the polluted air and degraded land finally gave rise to certain disasters, from soot in Port Harcourt to flooding in Benue and some other parts of the country, people lost their homes, health, and even lives. The usual response in situations like these is the government and various donor organizations appearing with relief materials and compensation, without putting any mitigating infrastructure.

With the population rising astronomically, the need to address poverty alleviation, and the current drive for industrialization and diversification of the economy, there will be pressure on the lands. The pressure on the lands should not stop us from putting back what we take from the land. We must not push the land to a state where it fights back, as we have seen in distant nations with their attendant weather crisis.

The state of the nation is a topic that widely interests the people in the country. We enjoy consuming news about our politics, our economy, our football, our entertainers, etc. Many of us are very passionate and never fail to engage in a discussion concerning these topics. One topic that I find missing in these discussions is the state of our environment. For the fact that the environment is the most important part of our lives, it should be at the forefront of our Newspaper publications, Television programs, and Radio broadcasts. We simply don't talk about the deteriorating state of our environment enough.

Northern Nigeria is dealing with some of the negative trends of adverse climate condition. This region is plagued by rising temperatures, which leads to the expansion of the Sahara into these settlements. The primary vocation of the people in these regions that are ravaged by desertification is Pastoral Herding. They are continually looking for greener pastures to feed their livestock, and in the absence of greenery, they are forced to migrate to other regions of the country to keep their herd alive. This migration from the northern region to the south and middle belt often result in clashes with farmers, as we often see in the news.

The southern region isn't exempt from adverse climate conditions. There has been an increase in the levels of rainfall which has caused severe floods and rising sea levels in some regions. The solution to the climate situation is more than awareness. As much as awareness can help to propagate the agenda, it needs to be done at the grassroots. We need to find a way to spread this information to the average Nigerian in a way that they can understand. Government policies need to be revised in such a way that prioritizes the environment. We don't have to wait until we have severe climate conditions to prioritize the land, or else the consequences of the adverse climate conditions will be very critical.

We have heard of mudslides with thousands of deaths; we have seen floods everywhere that damage homes, farmlands, and properties. Lately, we have also seen bushfires that have destroyed homes and towns. It's time to ask ourselves when it will be serious enough for us to act and demand action.

I will, therefore, summarise with a position that I have taken in my writings and lectures over the years and that is, we should never take more from the land than we have put back into it unless we will not be able to leave the land a better place than we met it, which will be such a shame.

Environmental Pollution: The Elephant In The Room

Nigeria's population has grown tremendously since its independence. Our landmass, on the other hand, has remained relatively constant. With an increase in population, there is also a proportional increase in human activities within our country. Sadly, human activities aren't always positive; thus, numerous human activities are currently putting a strain on our environment and affecting it negatively.

With a projected headcount of about 200 million people in less than ten years, it is fair to argue that our environment will feel the impact severely if we don't tame this wildfire before it spreads too far. We can already see the effects of environmental degradation caused by environmental pollution and with time, the situation will worsen unless we act fast.

When I think of environmental pollution, I think about a problem that has been overlooked for too long, crying for attention. Environmental pollution doesn't just affect us; it affects our farmlands, our marine life, and all elements that are necessary for survival on earth, such as water and air.

Lagos State is a city dear to my heart. I have lived in this city for as long as I can remember, and it saddens me to see the current state of the environment. Plastics has manoeuvred its way into our city and taken over our streets, our rivers and lakes, our lives. Our gutters are stagnant and home to various foreign elements. The foul smell given off by our gutters is so strong that one has no choice but to sacrifice breathing for a few seconds so as not to be impaled by the strong odour.

Why have we made such close allies with filth? It is a usual sight in Lagos to see heaps of refuse dumped right beside a waste bin. We clearly have a waste problem that needs to be tackled urgently. Improper management of our waste has tainted the aesthetic appeal of our beloved city and is a breeding ground for mosquitoes and other elements that are not beneficial to our health.

There is also the issue of street trading and hawking. These activities contribute to the heaps of waste that litter the city and the whole nation. Not to talk about the number of fumes being inhaled by these street traders or the fact that most of the street trading is used as a way to get rid of expired or soon to be expired goods by some shop owners. I have always campaigned against this common practice to the point where I raised the notion to charge the buyers, not the sellers, a fine as a way to curb hawking and roadside street trading.

The air we breathe is no stranger to pollution. Our cities are littered with tanker drivers who release thick black smoke from their exhaust into the atmosphere. Tanker drivers alone aren't to blame for increased air pollution. Our factories and industries, burning of fossil fuels, and indoor air pollution, also contributes handsomely to a polluted atmosphere. Gas flares from oil operation are extremely harmful to our atmosphere, and sadly, policies haven't been appropriately put in place to reduce these operations.

Though we cannot see the effects of air pollution, that doesn't mean they don't exist. Our Ozone Layer, which protects ecosystems on our planet, is depleting due to the effect of air pollution. Global warming is also caused by depletion of the Ozone Layer. Respiratory and heart problems can be directly traced to a polluted atmosphere, and unfortunately, we created these problems for ourselves.

Regardless of your social class, you are directly affected by the effects of air pollution. Air that is unsafe for breathing affects us equally.

The black soot in Port Harcourt was first noticed sometime around November 2016. Residents discovered that there is a cloud of soot above them, and it found its way into their lives and became a big problem. Social Media campaigns were started, and from the images and videos shared online, you could see that this wasn't a false alarm.

Residents couldn't help but notice that their feet would become black after walking barefoot around the house. Clothes become black after they've been left to dry on the line. It's been almost two years since our attention was brought to this issue, yet nothing has been done. Lives are at risk in these communities. Children are being born in these communities, and their quality of life will be affected if something is not done quickly.

Countries around the world have started to adopt renewable sources of energy and are slowly phasing out non-renewable sources of energy due to the effects on the environment. China has announced that it will ban production of petrol and diesel cars in the nearest future and I foresee other developed countries going down the same route.

Nigeria, on the other hand, is entertaining rumours of a proposed increase in import duty on solar panels. How is this the way forward? Why are we still heavily dependent on generators as our major source of power? Asides from the unbearable noise pollution, we are not doing our environment any good by normalizing the use of generators in the majority of our households.

According to Dike Okwelum, a medical expert and FADE volunteer, who graciously contributed to this piece. Since we share everything on earth with every living thing on the planet, what happens in one area affects everything no matter how far away. There are many kinds of pollution but the ones that have the most impact on health are air, water and noise pollution.

• Air, Water, and Noise Pollution

For air pollution, the level of effect is dependent on the length of time of exposure and the kind and concentration of chemicals and particles exposed.

Short-term effects are irritation of the eyes, nose, throat, upper respiratory infections like bronchitis, pneumonitis, eye inflammation like conjunctivitis. Others include headaches, nausea, anorexia, allergic skin reactions, and aggravation of medical condition in individuals with asthma, and emphysema.

Long-term effects are chronic cardiopulmonary diseases. Air pollutants are mostly carcinogenic and living in highly polluted areas puts people at risk of skin and lung cancer, as well as damage to the brain, nerves, liver, and kidneys in newborns.

Persistent coughing, wheezing is often observed among city folks in polluted areas. It is important to note that an increase in atmospheric temperature is directly proportional to an increase in air pollutants.

When exposure to carbon monoxide leads to blood carboxyhaemoglobin levels in the range of 3 to 10 percent, the effect will reduce work capacity in healthy young adults, aggravates angina symptoms during exercise, and impair mental vigilance. High levels will cause headaches, dizziness, fibrinolysis, and death. And in pregnant women, it reduces fetal birth weight, causes poor developmental milestone in the index child.

Dr. Okwelum further opines that another danger to watch out for is Lead Poisoning. In the general population, the major source of Lead is food and drink. In industries, inhalation of contaminated air may be more critical. The significant Lead sources in the environment are fuel additives released from automobile emissions and various industrial sources.

Lead is deposited near roads and in the vicinity of Lead smelters or where discarded batteries are burned. Other sources include Lead water pipes and tanks. Storage of food in Lead soldered cans or pottery in which Lead in the glaze and pigments have not been adequately stabilized. Children are particularly at risk if they chew and eat Lead-based paints from old houses or the soil around the homes.

The earliest effect of Lead poisoning is interference with the body's haemoglobin production leading to severe anaemias. Symptoms will include but not limited to fatigue, lassitude, generalized aches, muscle and joint pains, abdominal discomfort, and a bad taste in the mouth, as well as Kidney damage and encephalopathy in children.

Just like the air we breathe, water is vital to our survival. We need clean water to drink; we play in rivers, lakes, lagoons, and streams. Water is a precious resource that can be easily polluted. Polluted water can cause amebiasis, typhoid fever, severe gastroenteritis like cholera, and all forms of diarrhoea diseases.

Water contaminated with heavy metals like Lead, pesticides, hydrocarbons can cause hormonal and reproductive problems, damage to the nervous system, and some form of congenital disabilities in newborns.

Asides air and water pollution, another serious but often overlooked form of pollution is noise. Noise pollution is equally as dangerous as the rest, but sadly Nigeria has become accustomed to noise. Every evening in our homes, the sound of generators take over the whole street, and this has become so normalized that we don't pay attention to how much noise the generators are producing until they are turned off. During the day, we are constantly assaulted by blaring horns from other cars and sirens from cars escorting our so-called VIPs.

The cumulative impact of noise pollution can lead to hearing loss in a person over time. Noise pollution has been directly linked to tinnitus, stress and hypertension. It can also lead to building up aggression in a person, as well as other anti-social behaviours.

Summarily, I daresay we are overdue for a serious discussion with ourselves about our environment. We need to not only have this discussion but to make conscious efforts to change our lifestyle and do away with things that are affecting our environment negatively.

Generators: Killing Us and Killing the Environment

Some years ago, I listened to a television program at which a statistician responded to the reporter's question on the power situation in Nigeria. While I don't remember the complete response, but I clearly recall he stated that there must be about 50 million generators in Nigeria at the time. That figure stuck with me as I thought it was such a shame. Sadly, between then and now, we must be looking at double that number with no sign of reducing anytime soon. If in doubt, one only has to look around Victoria Island to confirm that in most homes and offices, there are at least two alternating generators. The same goes for homes and offices in Ikoyi, Lekki, Yaba, Surulere, Ikeja and many other areas in the city. If the generators do not vary in size and or capacity, they definitely vary in fuel consumption, all in a bid to strike a balance.

Nighttime in Lagos is a deafening affair as each home competes in a game of whose generator roars the loudest. There is also the issue of colouring the sky grey or black with exhaust fumes, depending on the state of the generator.

Not only Lagos that is affected by the inconvenience caused by generators; the same happens in all the major cities across the country. Silence and fresh air in urban areas across the country are luxuries many of us have come to learn to do without, albeit grudgingly.

As part of my work as an environmentalist, my team and I conducted some investigation on this matter. We found that though efforts are being made to bring the electricity situation in the country to a reasonable level, the business of importing, marketing generators and the fuel that goes with it has continued to expand. "Could it be that because of the revenue it generates, and the number of millionaires it has created, the efforts made by the government to ensure stable power may never come to fruition?" This is the question on the minds of many Nigerians.

It's quite disheartening to hear constantly that millions and billions have been sunk into the power sector, but no substantial change has occurred to our erratic power supply. Factually, apart from the Ministry of Petroleum, no other ministry has ever gotten as much funding as the Ministry of Power. For example, a whopping sum of 2.74 trillion Naira has been spent in attempts to improve power supply in Nigeria since 1999. That figure would have added up by now as this fact was disclosed in 2015 during the senate committee investigation of investments in the power sector in the 16 years of the PDP rule in Nigeria. Perhaps, there are some groups of individuals that will suffer a significant loss to their livelihood if the power sector is restored to a dependable state and we rid ourselves and our nation of these hazardous machinery that we have been forced to coexist with. Truthfully, there is a lot to be gained from a deplorable power sector. The enforced dependency of Nigerians on generators is enriching a group of people somewhere because 1 in 3 homes in Nigeria is partially dependent on generators which have to be fueled with petrol or diesel very frequently. I don't need to do the math for you to know that the recurring cost of running a generator can add up to hundreds of thousands per household in a year.

It's no wonder why there were and still are speculations surrounding the mysterious death of Late Attorney General of the Federation, Chief Bola Ige. One can't help but wonder how he was allegedly killed as the Minister of Power attempting to probe into the corruption in the power sector while he was in government. A probe that he had promised would finally ensure that Nigeria was on the right path to a constant power supply. He was famous for saying that he would end the nightmare of electricity supply in six months. Was the timing of his death unrelated to his attack on the power sector, or did he know something that eventually led to his untimely death? I guess only time can truly reveal the truth about his mysterious passing.

President Muhammadu Buhari recently mentioned that Obasanjo's government (PDP) spent close to $16 billion on the power sector with no reasonable result. The counter-argument to that statement made by Buhari is that the APC government has also spent close to $2 billion with only three years in office. With that being said, the APC government is following their predecessor in wasting our national budget on an ailing power sector.

Where is all that money going? Every year we turn a blind eye to the government's wasteful spending, which is clearly highlighted in the proposed national budget approved by the national assembly each year. We are so used to the government allocating huge amounts of money for the same thing year after year, and instead of maintaining these items, the government allocates funds to have them completely replaced. It appears that in the same fashion, the power sector has become the government's latest victim of the wasteful spending disease; just another vessel to siphon huge portions of our national budget for their own pockets.

The question every Nigerian should ask regarding this issue are the following:

- If the sum of $20 billion has been spent in less than 20 years, why is it that we still don't have power?

- Why has the government not been able to provide alternative sources of power at a cheaper rate?

In an effort to reduce the effect of carbon dioxide in the atmosphere, some state governors are planting tree corridors around the state. Sadly, on these same streets, we find street lights being powered by generators. The fumes from the generators are the leading cause of death of these trees.

With our investments in the power sector, we should be one of the top 10 leading nations in power generation. If the right investments were made, we should also have planned on relying less on non-renewable sources of energy to more renewable sources of energy. The world is leaving us behind. How is it possible for us to industrialize if we cannot provide something as simple as power?

We are blessed as a country with such resilient, innovative and resourceful people, which is why ordinary Nigerians have figured out a way to be less dependent on generators and our national grid. Nigerians have started to look into renewable sources of energy such as solar panels and inverters to store energy. Unfortunately, in the usual fashion, the efforts of the average Nigerian are being crippled by the selfish interest of a corrupt government. To frustrate the efforts of the average Nigerian, the federal government imposed a tariff on solar panels and inverters coming into the country.

The effect of generators on human life is disastrous. Starting from the polluted air that we breathe to a general discomfort from the excessive noise emanating from numerous generators at the same time. This is why an improvement in the quality of life in Nigeria means moving away from clustered neighbourhoods where the ruinous sound of generators begin at 7pm into the late night, to a more secluded area where you are far away from the noise of any generator.

Life Is Land: Towards A Cleaner Environment

I inhaled and exhaled with a smile when I stepped outside in the wee hours of the morning at the Mandela Gardens, Asaba; the air felt fresh and new. I took a seat and watched as ribbons of golden sunlight spilt through the trees. The trees were a black silhouette against the brilliant yellow sky. The dew drops, adorning the grass, seemed to glow with their own silvery radiance.

The yellow ball of sunlight started rising, as if from the ground; it filled the sky with mighty shades of yellow and splashed the clouds with endless rays of light. It was mesmerising, inviting me to stare, deep into the horizon, and bringing me into the bright dawn of one of the days I always look forward to each year: The day the world comes together to celebrate Mother Nature by highlighting issues that affect her the most and taking steps to address them.

As we celebrate the United Nations World Environment Day, June 5th 2018, I am particularly impressed by the theme ***"Beat Plastic Pollution."*** Slow, silent, omnipresent, ever-increasing, and more toxic than previously thought, the plastic pollution's reality bears sobering consequences that are only just getting the proper attention it deserves. As the world population continues to grow, and inevitably, the amount of garbage we produce, it is becoming evident that we now have front row seats to the greatest, most unprecedented' plastic waste tide ever faced.

A common description of plastic pollution is when plastic has gathered in an area and has begun to negatively impact the natural environment and create problems for plants, wildlife and even human population.

Plastic has only really existed for the last 60 to 70 years, but in that time it has become ubiquitous, transforming everything from clothing, cooking and catering, to product design, engineering and retailing. While its usefulness cannot be contested, it is also proven that plastics are composed of major toxic pollutants that have the potential to cause significant harm to the environment in the form of air, water and land pollution. Also, due to its durability, it is not biodegradable, which poses a big problem for the environment and its inhabitants. Nearly all the plastics ever created still exist in some form today.

As we all may know, there are many planets in the universe, Jupiter, Mars, Venus, etc., but science tells us that our Earth is the only planet with life. Various explorations of the rest of the planets show they do not have water, oxygen, rivers and oceans, trees and plants; therefore, no inhabitants or food. However, the debate is still ongoing in the scientific community on the possibility of life in other planets. As that has yet to be proven, it is clear that the destruction of earth will be the end of mankind. It comes to reason therefore that when the planet earth was created millions of years ago, the trees and shrubs, the rivers, the seas and the oceans were there before human beings and other inhabitants because we needed the oxygen, the air, and we needed the food to be able to survive.

It then becomes imperative to protect and nurture the very thing that ensures our existence. Sadly, that has not been the case, and the UN 2018 focus - plastic pollution, is just one of the many other man-made menaces threatening our existence. Quoting Mahatma Gandhi, *"to forget how to tend the soils and nurture the land is to forget ourselves."*

Alas, it is clear as day that we have forgotten ourselves. Statistics abound showing the damage plastic pollution has done to human life and the environment.

We don't have to look very far to witness the damaging effects of plastic on land. Around the nation, we see plastic in our gutters, impeding the flow of water waste and thereby causing blockages which ultimately result in flooding during the rainy season. On our farmlands, we see plastic sachet water wrappers hanging from trees as a result of the wind relocating them from the ground and onto tree branches.

Arguments abound that with the plastics on the ground, crops do not get the necessary nutrient from the land, seeing they have to compete with the plastics for these nutrients. Also, it's common knowledge that plastics contain harmful toxins that are released when exposed to heat; this is why it is advised not to consume water in plastic bottles that have been left in the car for too long. If toxins are released from plastic with exposure to heat, it then means that these same toxins are released into the land from where our food grows.

In essence, the phrase "Land is Life" has a deeper meaning because if truly land is life, the harmful things we do to our land directly affects our health. It's no wonder that the mortality rate for men and women in Nigeria is one of the lowest in the world. It affects us all equally, the rich and the poor, the young and the old. If harmful toxins are leaking into our land, we are consuming crops that grow from that land. If our animals are eating food that has been directly affected by one form of pollution or another, we are consuming these animals, and in the long run, we develop health problems that can eventually become fatal.

You are not any safer from the air pollution around just because you are sitting comfortably in your air-conditioned car or house, because the air that is filtered and recycled in the compressor is the same polluted air everyone else is breathing.

In developing an effective strategy for curbing plastic pollution in particular, we can take a clue from the cigarette campaign of many years ago which didn't put a full stop to the use but significantly reduced it. Many years ago, there was hardly any designated smoking spot, so people smoked anywhere and everywhere. That has changed, and smoking isn't even allowed in several places now.

Tackling the plastic waste problem needs a collective effort from everyone. There are many ways to address this problem from pushing for policies that ban plastic bags to establishing more recycling plants. In my own little way to commemorate the World Environment Day, FADE Africa brought together people from different walks of life to discuss the problem and also proffer solution. Wale Adebiyi of Wecyclers, talked about the need to imbibe the culture of recycling. School students made beautiful crafts from plastic waste, showing that treasure could be found in waste. Artists like Yelloseese and Odunayo Ajayi depicted artworks made from or about plastics, and Olusola Ajagbonna, a talented upcycling expert, taught on ways to upcycle our plastic waste.

I will conclude with this appeal by the Executive Director of the United Nations Environmental Programme (UNEP), Erik Solhiem: *"Making the switch from disposable plastic to sustainable alternatives is an investment in the long-term future of our environment."* It benefits us all.

How Little We Are

The ability to see the social, political, and economic value of caring for our environment appears to boil down to a question of intellectual humility. As the generations coming after look forward to living a better quality of life on earth, this lack of intellectual humility will harm us in ways we cannot begin to fathom, as many remain blind to the full implication of the issues we now face with climate change. We think we know it all, yet we know not, and thus, treat the warning signs and voices of wisdom about our environment with nonchalance.

We, in Nigeria and some neighbouring African countries have done little or nothing to seriously address the issues around mitigation against climate change. Our level of nonchalance on this issue is evident in this country, where I once asked myself in utter shock: How does a nation like Nigeria not have a Minister of Environment for any given period; is the Ministry of Environment jinxed? At every cabinet reshuffle, I would go to Abuja to welcome the new Minister of Environment, until the sixth one within a period of five years (2000 - 2005) when I eventually got tired and a bit too old for the frequency of those visits.

I must say, one of the nicest things that Gen. Olusegun Obasanjo did in 1999 on becoming the Commander in Chief of the Federal Republic of Nigeria was the creation, for the first time in Nigeria, the Ministry of Environment. Before then, it was the Environmental Protection Agency, a department in one of the ministries, until the middle of 1999 when the president appointed Ambassador Adamu Wakili Adamawa, who was then our Ambassador in Washington, as the Minister of Environment.

I had known the Ambassador, and we met and related in Atlanta during the 1966 Olympics, as a humanist and nature-loving man. I had gone on to produce a working paper for him during his brief stay as the Honourable Minister. I fondly recall a reception with him in Abuja where the Master of Ceremonies introduced him as Mr. Environment. In his speech, he not only acknowledged me but added that *"if there is anybody that deserved the title of Mr. Environment, it would be Dr. Newton Jibunoh because of what he was doing on the Environment."* I had just returned to

Nigeria then after the Solo drive from Lagos to London, and the expedition was well reported by NTA, CNN, and BBC. However, after Ambassador Adamu as Minister, there were four succeeding ministers of a critical Ministry of Environment every other year. Thus, I had to ask myself in utter shock, how does a nation like Nigeria go for that long without a Minister of Environment? How will issues like the cleanup campaign in Ogoni land, desertification and erosion and its hostile encroachment on the coastal and riverine areas of the country be tackled? These are things that two Ministers will work hard to realize, talk less of having none. Vulnerable farmers and citizens will pay dearly for climate change if we continue this way.

The seriousness of climate change is evident in how much it has occupied and unsettled global communities in the last few years. I shared stories from the desert warrior initiative that was designed to become part of the blueprint for mitigating against desertification and the migration of people and animals living on the fringes of the desert. The initiative would have been beneficial in restoring greenery to the 11 frontline states in Nigeria and other areas on the fringes of the desert. This would have helped farmers by improving the fertility of the soil, thereby improving the livelihood of millions of people. It was also meant to teach people about land management and land reclamation. To think that this whole idea started about 20 years ago, and if it was followed through as was designed, we could have averted the catastrophes that we predicted and now see taking place.

I recall briefing some of the governors at that time, but I suspect that by telling them that most of the initiative would take between 20 to 30 years to realize, which would be long after their tenure, I couldn't convince most of them to adopt the concept for their states. The thought of continuity and delayed gratification aren't concepts many of our leaders have managed to grasp fully. I, however, do not regret doing so, as the truth is most climate actions would take more than four years to realize, and from studies carried out on other deserts, the extent of land reclamation required to tame the Sahara would take over 20 years.

The Sahara is the largest hot desert in the world with an area of 9,200,000 square kilometres which is comparable to the area of China or the United States. My findings and knowledge of the terrain, which is slightly different from other deserts like the Gobi desert and the Negev desert, informed the content of my initial briefing to the government, and all that led to proving how little we are for not understanding nature. I cannot stop wondering about how much nature has given us and how little it has received in return. There is a quote that says, *"if all mankind were to disappear, the world would regenerate back to the rich state of equilibrium that existed ten thousand years ago, but if insects were to vanish, the environment would collapse into chaos."* For such a tiny part of the entire ecosystem, humans have contributed the most to its deteriorating state. The world's 7.6 billion people only represent just 0.01% of all living things on earth.

Take for example in a Tsunami, some marine and land animals may die, but mostly, humans will die and suffer for it because we depend hugely on our infrastructure whereas every other player in the ecosystem only needs nature to thrive. In a wildfire, we may lose some trees and a few animals, but many humans will burn and lose properties that will take years to rebuild both physically and financially. And in the case of desertification, yes, humans will suffer the most from famine, drought, and all other effects that come with it. In other words, we stand the most to lose if we continue to destroy the infrastructure provided by nature.

As a boy, we were taught to catch an animal commonly referred to as *"Bushmeat"* from the forest because if we didn't, they would reproduce in large numbers overpopulating the bushes, overrunning the farms and destroying valuable crops, making them a threat to our food security. Of course, the fact that it was a delicacy in the soups eaten in many homes was rarely mentioned as a reason. We would set traps around my father's plantation to catch them not caring about the role they may be playing in the plantation. We believed that we were doing nature a service due to what we were told about the animal. The same goes for the fishes we caught in the rivers which we were told could lay thousands of eggs in one minute, so we needed to catch them to prevent overpopulation. Today, we seem to catch both the fish and their eggs, with no thought or consideration for reproduction and replenishment for continuity of life; how little we are.

Becoming an environmentalist over 40 years ago and studying the effect these animals have on our biodiversity, I have had to change my position and now campaign against the incessant killing of animals for food. I have been extremely fortunate to have been exposed at a very early age to farming around the big forests, to hunting expeditions, and travelling with fishermen through big rivers on fishing expeditions. Although our elders didn't always have the best understanding of certain things in nature, they had a love for it and at that tender age, so did I. Nature has been a part of my life for a very long time. I have also been able to realise that when we reject nature, it is like we are rejecting life and all the good things that come with it. Thus, by destroying nature, we are in one way or the other destroying lives because nature has a way of coming back to hurt us, as recently seen around many parts of the world.

The floods are getting more frequent and intense, causing immense damage to lives and properties like with the case of Cyclone Idia in Mozambique and two neighbouring countries. In California, wildfires are becoming a regular occurrence. Migration is on the rise as people are losing their farmlands; hence, their source of income, leading to massive migration of farmers, herders and people looking for a better life. Insecurity is also booming as organisations seeking to wreak havoc in the land find easy targets for recruitments in young people now rendered idle and poor due to lack of farms and herds to tend. The ripple effect is far-reaching and needs to be addressed.

We, humans, are so big in our developments with our big and thinking brains but so little when considering our relationship with other creatures that share the earth with us by showing little respect with the way we catch and eat them - sometimes raw, sometimes fried, and sometimes cooked. We constantly disregard nature's infrastructure that is meant to create balance in the ecosystem. Take, for instance, the nest that the birds and other similar animals build all over, on trees, shrubs, and grass; these nests serve as their homes. Once we cut down all our trees, shrubs and grasses; we leave the birds with no place to build their homes and lay their eggs. Also, take the islands that nature provided for migrating animals as a stopover to rest when moving from one continent to another. Once we turn all our islands into retreats and housing estates; the migrating animals won't find anywhere to rest as they travel; thereby, reducing the rate at which they migrate, and sadly, also their lives due to the strain of the journey. Take the houses that the ants build with unique architecture with compartments completed in recorded time. Take the fish that mate and lay eggs underneath the riverbeds, ocean beds and sea beds. We show them very little care, let alone respect.

As part of my obsession to check environmental degradation like incriminating human waste disposals, cutting down trees and vegetation without replenishing, and the careless disposal of plastics, FADE Africa decided to pay a visit to some motor parks to enlighten them about the health consequences of many habits that are very common in motor parks. We sought to enlighten them on the dangers of the lack of a proper waste disposal system, lack of toilets to dispose their bodily waste instead of doing it out in the open and the general hygiene of the park. We also enlightened them about noise pollution from incriminating use of their horns.

Many of them couldn't imagine driving without honking, so I told them a story of driving from Lagos to London for five weeks without using my horn once. At the initial stage of our discussion, they showed very little interest until I shared my story of driving without honking. From then, we secured their attention, and as such, we were able to let them know that most of them may not live to be sixty and even if they do, they would have lost their hearing, their eyesight or be in an overall unhealthy state because the environment they live and work in daily is heavily degraded. Science may be able to find us an alternative to foods like GMOs, but they won't be able to find us alternative air to breathe that is affordable - free.

The Present Global Climate Must Be Too Cold for Donald Trump

Like the sword of Damocles, much controversy hovered over the United States President, Donald Trump. His face became constantly plastered on our TV screens, newspapers, and other media outlets since the day he declared his interest in the US presidency. An interest he eventually realized. Unfortunately, the majority of the news concerning Donald Trump that makes the headlines aren't always good news.

One of the first things he did after becoming president was to pull America out of the Paris Agreement. An agreement that as of May 2018, 195 United Nations Framework Convention on Climate Change (UNFCCC) members had signed and 177 members are party to. The long-term goal of this agreement is to keep the annual increase in global average temperature well below 2°C above the preindustrial level temperatures.

China and the United States happen to be the principal parties of this agreement. Being the biggest polluter, America's former president, Barrack Obama, was the first to sign followed by China; President Buhari (Nigeria) also signed in September 2016.

• The Importance of The Paris Agreement

The Paris Agreement was a milestone achievement for the world and those fighting to ensure we still have one. The Agreement defines a universal, legal framework to strengthen the global response to the threat of climate change. It requires all involved to make contributions to climate change mitigation by developing plans on how to make these contributions and communicate their plans to the Secretariat of the convention.

The agreement aims, in the long run, to limit the increase in global warming to 1.5°C starting in 2020, as well as achieve net-zero emissions in the second half of the century. Another important goal of the agreement is to increase the ability to adapt to the adverse impact of climate change in a manner that doesn't threaten food production.

Most of the countries that were passionate about the environment attended various meetings over the course of the inception of the agreement because it was clear that if nothing was done to lower the global temperature, the consequences in the not distant future would lead many of the vulnerable countries to experience some severe or catastrophic weather change. So, when Donald Trump, as a presidential candidate, said if he became president, he would withdraw from the Paris Agreement deal, some of us didn't take him seriously because we were sceptical about him winning the presidency. Our scepticism lingered even after he became president because we thought it would be insane for him to pull out of the deal.

If the United States carries on with its present stand on the Paris Agreement, the rest of the participating countries may need to revisit and renegotiate aspects of the agreement. America played a significant role in crafting and pushing forward the agreement, and as of today, the global temperatures have continued to rise because of global warming and climate change. The good news is that despite Trump, many states, scores of cities, institutions and companies in the United States of America have pledged to meet or surpass the standards set by President Obama to reduce America's global warming potentials by 26 percent by the year 2025 from their levels in 2005 (https://nyti.ms/2suoYdl).

The science of Global Warming is now incontrovertible. Trump and the Republican doubters are nothing but clogs in the wheel of change, whose interest lies only in the profits that big businesses will declare for their shareholders, even while the earth fries from their pollution. Island nations and many low-land countries that are below sea level will suffer from severe flooding with the occurrence of coastal disasters and severe weather phenomena.

In the drylands and Sahel regions, there will be desertification and bush fires from rising temperatures and drought. And in Nigeria, regions like Benue, Lagos, Asaba, Warri, Eket, Port Harcourt, etc. that are built on flood plains will experience very catastrophic climate disasters.

Some of us remember the first time an atomic bomb was used on Hiroshima, Japan. That was the first time an atomic bomb exploded in any part of the world. The second exploded in Nagasaki three days later. More than 50 years after this devastating incident, the effect it had on climate change and the people of Japan is still evident today. There was almost another barrage between the Soviet Union and the USA over Cuba but was averted when Nikita Khrushchev, heading the ultimatum of John F. Kennedy, pulled back the Russian ships laden with nuclear-tipped missiles that were headed for Cuba in 1962.

Why am I mentioning these? I feel the need to remind ourselves of these because since that time, for more than 50 years, all American Presidents continued to hold Cuba as number one enemy of the state, until President Obama started the process of normalizing the relationship between the USA and Cuba. President Donald Trump has decided to roll back this agreement too, thereby heating up the world political sphere.While all these are happening, he is still pursuing his regime change policies in countries like Yemen, Syria and Venezuela.

Other notable changes which affects the environment that President Trump has made since being President include:

- **Pulling out of the Iran Nuclear Deal:** Just recently, President Donald Trump decided to pull the United States out of the Iran Nuclear Deal drafted after years of negotiations by the P5 +1 Countries. So far, this deal has been one with the best potential of being a model to curb the spread of nuclear weapons anywhere in the world. According to

Trump, he pulled out of the deal because it is "decaying and rotten" and is an embarrassment to him as a citizen of the United States. President Trump vows to re-impose economic sanctions that were waived when the deal was signed in 2015. Pulling out of this deal, America risks increasing regional tension, enabling the further spread of nuclear weapons and the possibility of another Middle Eastern war, something that Netanyahu, the Prime Minister of Israel desires.

• **Recognizing Jerusalem as the capital of Israel:** In a bid to advance the Middle East peace process, as dubious an approach as it sounds, President Trump recognized Jerusalem as the capital of Israel. He has since then relocated the US embassy from Tel-Aviv, the former capital, to Jerusalem. Many world leaders have frowned upon this move, citing that the move will constitute a flagrant provocation of Muslims all over the world, tending toward war.

President Donald Trump policy changes will cause a catastrophic ripple effect if not handled properly. His tactic appears to be using the threat of war to achieve peace or acquiescence. That is bullying. If care is not taken, these policy changes might lead to a third world war which may leave our world as we know it, in ruins. Vulnerable countries, such as Nigeria, will be the biggest losers.

The JCPOA heralded the Iran Nuclear treaty negotiated by the US, Britain, Russia, China, France, and Germany. With the unilateral abandonment by the US, Trump will have to impose sanctions on Iran and those doing business with Iran. That will pit America against its allies in the West, China, and Russia, all of whom have no desire to see the deal torpedoed. It is highly probable that if these countries stick together, they will frustrate Trump's sanctions. Then what? Trump may then be forced to go to war to create another batch of dead Americans to whom the US will be grateful for their freedom. The weapons manufacturers and merchants will get richer supplying arms to various factions; Russia, China, and the US will arm opposing sides to the teeth, and the country or region that is the theatre of war gets devastated.

With any luck, such sanctions may just necessitate only trade wars with allies, the likes of which will devastate world economies. We already have NAFTA in animated suspension. America's embargo with Cuba is off and on; in a confused state. North Korea has itchy fingers and will love to take on a weakened US. Then what? Will Trump unleash the nuclear weapons, or intimidate all to submissions? The last is not a likely option. The world of Donald Trump is chaotic and still not warm enough for him.

PART VII

THE LOSSES

"Where justice is denied, where poverty is enforced, where ignorance prevails... neither persons nor property will be safe."

— Frederick Douglas

Illegal Migration and Human Trafficking: The Failure of Humanity

Illegal migration and human trafficking have become a worldwide industry that employs millions of people and leads to the annual turnover of billions of dollars every year. More often than not, flourishing routes for these activities are made possible by weak legislation, lax border controls, corrupted public officers, and the power of the organised crime. Naturally, poverty, ignorance and warfare are major drivers to the rising tide of illegal migration and human trafficking.

The plague of human trafficking and illegal migration is the exploitation of man by man. Both of these threaten not just individuals but the foundational values and the strength of nationhood. It should keep us up at night wondering at the horrors many of our fellow human beings are facing at the exact moment we lie comfortably in our beds. Though different by definition, as while illegal migrants pay smugglers to assist them in crossing the borders, victims of trafficking are forced, coerced or deceived for the purpose of exploiting them; both are exploitative and illegal, and often have disastrous consequences for both the trafficked and the illegal migrant.

My first encounter with smugglers and illegal migrants occurred during one of my desert expeditions and that experience completely traumatised me. I still recall the incident like it was yesterday, when I stood on the deck of a ship I had boarded to transport my car which I had earlier driven across the desert from Nigeria to London on a second solo voyage.

There were possibly over a hundred migrants on deck, many in clusters laughing and chatting. I could overhear snippets of different conversations in Igbo and Yoruba, so I knew a number of my fellow countrymen were on board with me. As I stood gazing at the sky and breathing in the fresh air, a security officer with the ship walked up to me to ask for my documents. I easily presented them to him as I was always carrying them around, even when asleep. After showing him my documents, I was immediately advised to return to my cabin, which I had left in search of fresh air as my roommate was bent on smoking the night away. Sensing something was amiss, I complied. Decades later, I am still thankful to my Creator for my prompt obedience.

A few hours later, I stepped out of my cabin, in response to the announcement that car owners should go to their cars since the ship was about to dock. You see, not everyone on board the vessel has a cabin due to the extra cost it attracts, despite the 12-hour overnight journey across the Mediterranean Sea, so you can understand my surprise when I stepped out of my cabin to meet an empty deck. I knew the ship didn't have enough cabins to contain the hundreds of people I had seen earlier, and no one had gotten off yet since we were just getting close to the port. I saw the same security man that had met me before, and out of curiosity, I asked about the others; his next words still cause a chill to run down my spine whenever I remember it. He replied that they had been thrown overboard and I was lucky to be alive. At first, I thought it was a joke. How could that be? Seeing my confusion, he explained to me that they had received a tip that the ship was to be raided by Spanish port authorities and would have been seized if illegal immigrants were found on it. Thus, to prevent exposure as a ship being used by smugglers to move people illegally across the sea from Africa to Europe, the illegal migrants had to go; all drowned in the sea. On that day, hundreds of people died for nothing; they died because the crew didn't want to lose their ship. They were utterly wasted because some people who had willingly collected their money to smuggle them to Europe felt their lives didn't matter.

That is the reality of illegal migration and human trafficking in whatever form. It is the gross disregard of human life for profit.

• Factors Fueling Human Trafficking and Illegal Migration in Nigeria

With the release of the CNN footage of West Africans being sold at slave markets in Libya, and a more recent report about the situation in Nigeria's human trafficking hub, Edo State, also one of Africa's largest departure points, human trafficking has generated wild outrage globally.

Following calls for action, the Nigerian Government made strong statements on tackling the problem by improving the mechanisms for apprehending and convicting traffickers. The recent arrest of two officers of the Nigeria Immigration Service for attempted human trafficking through the Murtala Muhammed International Airport, Ikeja, Lagos, shows a certain level of commitment by the agencies involved in addressing this problem. But it will take a lot more than these arrests and curses by traditional rulers to curb the booming nature of this trade. There is a need to understand why people risk their lives to embark on the perilous journey of crossing the Sahara and Mediterranean Sea. True, the most obvious reason is a depressed economy. The appeal of greener pastures on the other side is strong enough for many to risk their lives. However, there are other areas to pay attention to, and these are:

- **Inability to Secure Legal and Safe Passage Out of the Country:** The difficulties of getting visas due to lack of adequate documentation often leave many desperate, forcing them to seek alternative means of leaving the country.

- **Domestic Syndicate Centres:** Traffickers have centres for screening and engaging their victims across the country, namely: Lagos, Edo, Delta, Onitsha and Aba. The centres serve as recruitment venues for traffickers to scout for potential victims, be it for smuggling goods or human trafficking. These agents prey on the desire of the victims to fend for themselves and their families, and or to escape tough situations. We need to find these centers and shut them down.

- **So-called success stories:** The traffickers deceitfully showcasing the less than 10 percent that actually make it across the Sahara and Mediterranean Sea; people who are sending money to their families from Italy and other countries.

- **Nigeria's Porous Borders:** This is one area that cannot be overemphasized. Our borders are badly exposed. People can easily get into the country as we see in the cases of nomadic herdsmen, and in the same vein, people can easily get out of the country. Nigeria offers passports to almost any West African national seeking one, which is not the case in other countries. This makes it very difficult for us to know who is coming in and who is leaving, which affects our ability to produce accurate data on the actual population of Nigeria, and the real Nigerians.

• The Way Forward: Solutions

It will take a concerted effort by the Federal and State Governments, and other stakeholders to cause serious damage to the multi-billion dollar criminal industry. For a start, I believe that there needs to be a nationwide grassroots campaign that will sensitize members of different communities about the ills of illegal migration. However, awareness is not enough. The government needs to look into the following suggested solutions:

- **Economic Empowerment:** This goes without saying that we need to grow our economy, or we will keep losing people to the desert and the sea.

- **Safe Camps for Returnees:** The government will need to do more than just rescue people from Libya or wherever they are, to actually resettle them back home. This is best done in a controlled space for a while under strict monitoring. This will help prevent a repeat performance from many of the returnees. Plantations can be set up for them to work in and get paid for the work.

- **Firmer Border Security:** There is need to secure the borders as most of these traffickers use the road network to move their victims. We can stop them before they even get out of the country. This needs to be the first point of control against illegal immigration.

- **Reorientation of the Masses:** This will entail a massive nationwide campaign to educate people on the ills of human trafficking and illegal migration, the forms they take, such as the offer of fake modelling contracts in Europe, schooling, etc. The hope is to deter people, including parents and relatives from voluntarily giving up their children or encouraging them to go to Europe illegally.

Summarily, human trafficking and illegal migration should matter to everyone; we cannot continue to look the other way and remain silent about things that matter; this is where we miss the whole point. No truer words capture my stance on this than a quote by the Former US President, Barack Obama, when he said, *"It ought to concern every person because it is a debasement of our common humanity. It ought to concern every community because it tears at our social fabric. It ought to concern every business because it distorts markets. It ought to concern every nation because it endangers public health and fuels violence and organized crime. I'm talking about the injustice, the outrage, of human trafficking, which must be called by its true name - modern slavery."*

The Shame of the Nation: 20th Century Human Trafficking and Slavery

All over the world, millions are held against their will for a crime committed against them. These are part of the world's population deceived, captured, dehumanised, and sold like goods, while the perpetrators rake in billions off the broken backs, broken hearts, and broken dreams of their victims, young and old. This act is a crime against humanity and a fundamental violation of human rights. It degrades and diminishes the whole human family and undermines the dignity of the human person.

That is the face of human trafficking. It is shamefully monstrous that human trafficking or let's call it by its real name, "slavery", persists in many corners of the world, exploiting an estimated 40 million people worldwide. Slavery may have long been officially outlawed and universally condemned, but as difficult as it may be to believe, numerically there are more slaves today than at any time in history. Make no mistake about it; it lurks everywhere waiting to pounce on its prey. According to a United Nations report, *"Every country is affected by human trafficking, whether as a country of origin, transit, or destination for victims."*

In more recent past, it took the power of CNN to bring the attention of our nation, Nigeria and the global community to the dehumanising treatment and sale of our citizens in Libya. The national outcry and the global condemnation of the Libyan authorities following the CNN documentary which exposed the activities of human traffickers and the plights of the trafficked, prompted our government to take action. The Nigeria government sent state functionaries, private planes, and other government support systems to Libya on a rescue mission to bring back some of the Nigerians that were being prepared for sale to the highest bidder.

The fate of these rescued Nigerians would have been different if the international community didn't raise awareness around this issue and force the government to step in. That, in itself, is quite disheartening for many others who are still lost or have died in the process because they were not fortunate enough to have the media shine a light on their plight. My colleagues and I were privileged to host some of the returnees and as may be expected, there was a lot of disorientation and hopelessness emitting from them. Who can blame them? No human being can be the same after being through a series of trauma like these migrants have. Is life in Nigeria that unbearable that our brothers and sisters are willing to cross through hell just to have a taste of heaven? How do you tell someone who doesn't know where their next meal is coming from to see a silver lining? Despair and hopelessness in the heart of a man can drive him to do unimaginable things. Sadly, the Nigerian state is the despair in the hearts of many of our citizens. That is why we are witnessing an exodus of our citizens to Europe, which started many years ago.

I analysed and debated this issue over and over with my colleagues to no comforting answers. I have a few problems about this whole matter because as far back as 2002, I wrote about how our countrymen and women were being treated overseas in their quest for greener pastures. Some dying in the desert (which I saw), some drowning in the Mediterranean (which I witnessed) and some being occasionally pushed aboard any vessel that didn't want to be captured for smuggling illegal immigrants to Europe.

Over the years, the Mediterranean and the Sahara,

aided by men in some cases, have taken the lives of too many Nigerian men and women trying to get across to Europe in search of greener pasture. It was discovered that out of about a hundred people who pay and begin the process of travelling to these greener pastures, only about 10 of them ever get through to their destination.

In our advocacy, my team and I have pointed out the need to investigate the cities and towns in this country where the international cartels have their offices. These traffickers have centres for screening and engaging their victims across the country: Lagos, Edo, Delta, Anambra and Abia. We have also indicated time and again how Nigeria's porous borders serve as another avenue encouraging human trafficking. Our borders are badly exposed. People can easily get into the country, as we see in the cases of nomadic herdsmen, and in the same vein, people can easily slip out of the country. This makes it very difficult for us to know who is coming in and who is going out, which affects our ability to accurately produce data on the true population of Nigeria and Nigerians.

Nonetheless, the good news that came out of the whole Libya human trafficking saga is the way the Federal Government responded in a very efficient manner. Thus, I commend the Federal Government for staying on top of the issue while it was going on. The Federal Government also put the might of the Presidency behind the rescue effort. The ministerial personnel also got involved as the Minister of Foreign Affairs actually made a trip down to Libya. The rehabilitation infrastructures that were put in place in Lagos, Abuja, and Benin are also some highlights of this rescue operation. We are told some of the returnees have been enrolled in skill acquisition programs, and some have become involved in the various campaigns to discourage this horrible affair.

However, even as we commend the government's effort and the numerous institutions involved, we have to emphasise on the need for a continued effort that looks at the big picture, not just the present. Sadly, this is one area that is still lacking; hence, I'm led to highlight the bad news. The bad news being that very little has been done to prosecute some members of the cartel responsible for the illegal migration and human trafficking of our brothers and sisters. There are not enough preventive measures put in place to put an end to this nightmare. We say this because some of the returnees have gone back to patronize these cartels in hopes that they finally achieve their dreams of crossing over into Europe. These cartels have been around for so long and have become multi-million dollar organizations heavily dependent on the naivety of these migrants.

The focus of the world has been on Libya, which is probably assumed to be the only place where these illegal activities are carried out. However, as mentioned earlier, this is not the case because there are similar camps or operations in Morocco, Algeria, and every corner of the world, no country is exempt. I have had the opportunity to visit one of these camps outside Nigeria accompanied by a Nigerian official to see the state that hundreds of these migrants were living in.

In an attempt to get involved, my organisation, FADE, offered to bring back one of these migrants whom we encountered. The migrant, impregnated in the camp after an assault by either a fellow migrant or a trafficker (she had no idea as she was raped in the dark), blatantly refused to return to Nigeria with us, despite our offer to cover her expenses. She preferred a bleak and hopeless life in the migrant camp to the shame and trouble she will face with the family, who sold everything to get her on this path of sorrow and misery. She believed she still stood a better chance of making it to Europe someday and building a 'good' life for her unborn child than she did if she returned home to Nigeria. Unfortunately, she is one of many who have been brainwashed to believe this is true.

Summarily, we must, essentially, put in place some kind of orientation programme in the communities where some of these migrants come from. The people in these communities should be informed about the skeletons of our sons and daughters scattered all over the Sahara. I believe that the young men and women that have been pushed overboard into the Mediterranean Sea and drowned for the fish to feed on will want us to tell their stories to deter their brothers and sisters from making the same mistake they made. Our girls and boys enslaved in prostitution all over Europe, who have become sub-humans due to the weight of abuse their bodies have suffered, should serve as an example to the young ones at home fantasizing about an illegal future in Europe.

It is pertinent that we communicate this information to the people of these communities so that they know that those members of their families that have embarked on such journeys may never be seen again. During our investigation on this topic, we encountered families that told us about their sons and daughters that left some years ago and never heard from them since. How do we tell them that some of those skeletons we saw in the desert could be their family member? Or that they could be among those that drowned trying to cross the Mediterranean? Or those that were pushed over could also be members of their families?

Human trafficking is a global phenomenon in the 21st Century in more hidden and clandestine ways, such as child labour, forced labour, bonded labour, and sexual exploitation. This is the reality, even though international instruments have long been created to regulate the rights and duties of individuals and society. Thus, human trafficking, as well as illegal migration, should absolutely matter to everyone, without exception.

Arts, Monuments, and Our Future: Chasers of The Lost Arts

Growing up into my early teens, I witnessed severally, the conversions of our so-called heathens to Christianity. It involved, in part, the burning of any graven image or artwork found in the household of the convert. Often the missionaries would leave with some of these images in a rucksack, announcing that those will have to be disposed of specially; perhaps, after serious prayers of intervention. Years later, as a student in England, I came to find similar artworks in the British Museums and homes of my European colleagues who had at one time or the other lived in Nigeria.

Africa, and especially West Africa, had been home to a great many Kingdoms. These included the Nok, Ife, Benin, Ancient Ghana, Mali, Songhai, Bush Valley and Asante kingdoms. They all grew wealthy trading in precious metals and farm produce. Additionally, the people of West Africa were skilled potters, sculptors, and metalworkers, using wood, brass, bronze, and gold in their works. Their art, especially in Benin, Ife, and Nok Kingdoms, were used to glorify their kings, deities, culture, wars, and celebrations. Early on in our march through history, our people had no knowledge of putting events and stories down on paper. But they told their stories in carvings on wood, stones, bronze, brass, etc. With the arrival of the Europeans who came first as traders, the 19th Century was particularly bad for the surviving kingdoms of West Africa. The declarations of Benin as a British Colony in 1897 and Asante also as one in 1902, effectively ended the era of the West African Kingdoms. These were quickly followed in 1914 with the amalgamation of the Southern Nigerian Colony and the Northern Nigeria Protectorate.

All over Africa, the Colonial Masters treated their colonies as conquered territories, yet there were no wars declared, except in pretence by the invading 'explorers'. The colonialists, thus, plundered and carted away numerous treasures, from artworks to resources and human beings. Whereas they made a show of paying (meagerly and immorally) for the resources and the humans shipped off, they brazenly stole the artworks through orchestrated smuggling and fake religious conversions. However, following the independence of these nations from the European colonising countries, African nations began to demand the return of their stolen treasures.

Now, fast-forward to the preparations of FESTAC 77 hosted by Nigeria; the government appointed a committee to locate and return to Nigeria all documented and historical works of art from anywhere in Europe and the Americas. The committee selected the Ivory mask of Queen Idia of Ancient Benin Kingdom as the festival symbol and offered two million pounds (£2,000,000) to the British government for the loan of this mask that sits in the British Museum following their refusal to return the mask. The British government rejected this offer to the chagrin of all decent people. By the end of Festac 77, that committee was disbanded. Since then, Nigeria has relied on the approach of quiet diplomacy to press for the recovery of its stolen history. Such quiet diplomacy had more or less been a colossal failure until recently with the announcement that the British Museum will be 'leasing' our work to us in the coming years.

The reasons for the previous failures and the pyrrhic victory are not farfetched. Firstly, during and after the festival, up until 1999, Nigeria was a 'militarised' country (except for a brief period between 1979-1983) with the military governments playing musical chairs with governance. The country under such rules had not shown any consistency in policy. The military government that came into power in 1975 almost cancelled the Festac festival. Secondly, there was no responsible body to take up the fight on the part of Nigeria following the dissolution of the first committee. The people in power had different priorities with each new government of the day, and so adequate attention was not given to matters of our history. One can easily argue that the authorities were inadvertently engaged in re-writing our history. Thirdly, Nigeria had been proving beyond doubt that she cannot manage her affairs. Museums set up in virtually every region were dying from neglect, poor staffing, low wages, low morale, and inadequate funding. The problem of poor management can still be seen in the poor documentation of our art treasures and resources to date. The British burned down the city of Benin in 1897, and so erased most of the records held in the kingdom. What they didn't burn down, they carted away or systematically destroyed. But those wanton acts have not stopped the British from reasoning that we are incapable of taking care of what's ours.

One good thing, amongst many others, about Nigerians though, is that we are an indefatigable people; a good number of us are. Citizens and groups have on their own kept on the fight for the return of our stolen history. Individuals, art lovers, cities and states have been able to trace most of the missing arts to most European and American cities. A lot of these are in private homes. Others are held in public view. However, we do not have a list of these works anywhere, comprehensive or otherwise. I believe that if there exists a standing committee tasked with the recovery of our art, the committee can easily set up such a data bank for effective dialogue with the looters.

I run a private museum in Lagos and have my works properly documented both digitally and in prints. This is constantly updated as I acquire more works. The irony is that I did this with the help of curators from the National Museum. So, we do have the talents. In 2001, there was a move between my museum, Didi Museum and the National Museum to digitalise their records and update them regularly. Due to lack of funding, that collaboration did not come to fruition. It may have been excusable that we could not write in the 17th and 18th centuries, but how can we defend our inability to manage our resources, our treasures, and document our history today - the 21st Century? We are making history every day of our lives. As I write, our present artists, sculptors, and metal workers are creating contemporary arts, some of which are truly iconic. Are we documenting these? Some of these works are in private hands, and the National Museum Commission may not have records of them. Elsewhere, it is not uncommon for Museums to acquire iconic works for historical purposes. Or lease them for exhibition permanently or from time to time. Who is documenting the works of our activist artists over time? Works of people like Dele Jegede, Jossy Ajiboye, Kenny Adamson, Fela Anikulapo-Kuti and Gani Fawehimi have all contributed to our present political landscape. We need to preserve such records, no matter how unpalatable they might be to some.

The Oba of Benin, Eheneden Erediauwa Omo N'Oba Ewuare II, called on the Prince of Wales, Prince Charles and his wife, during their October 2018 visit to Nigeria, to implore the British Government to return all Nigerian artworks, especially the Benin artworks held in Britain. A Museum is currently being built in Benin for the repository of Benin artworks. The British Government agreed on a three-year plan to "loan" some of the works to the Museum for exhibitions. Whilst this is an insult really, it is a positive shift from the British position in 1977.

In recent times also, there has been renewed clamour, albeit from unexpected quarters, for the restitution of the wrongs the colonialists had done to African nations. The President of France, Mr. Emmanuel

Macron, called on European nations to return all stolen arts and treasures to their African countries, starting with France. This welcome development will not be easy to achieve, though. But we must seize this opportunity to pursue this path to restitution vigorously.

Most importantly, these two developments underline the need to have a powerful standing committee for the recovery of Nigerian works of art anywhere they may be found in the world. Such a committee must be adequately funded at all times, empowered with diplomatic passports and credentials from the highest seat of our nation's government. The committee must not be politicised, must be made up of citizens with impeccable characters, who are apolitical, beyond reproach, and morally conscientious. They will need to be respected by, and comfortable around their hosts, for they must speak with candour and justice. It will be a long fight but fight we must.

If we must learn how to properly govern ourselves once more, we may need to step back a little into our past development, history and previous passed laws. We must also do it fast.

Arts, Monuments, and Our Future: Our Monuments of Old Are No More

Arts and monuments are a people's cultural heritage; always products of their time bearing tales to lend understanding to the future, and they are also reflections of power. The destruction and looting of cultural heritage have been intertwined with conflict for thousands of years. To steal an enemy's treasures, defile their sacred places and burn their cities has been part of war throughout history. But how do you explain a time where war was neither declared nor fought, yet destruction and looting of a people's cultural heritage abound, leaving a historical and cultural loss of unprecedented scale?

Long before the coming of the "mini gods" commonly known as colonial masters, our various kingdoms with their cities, towns, and villages had their places of reverence and sanctuaries of different forms.

These forms took the shape of king palaces, homes of deities, shrines, city walls and defences, and important streams. These were monuments for the people. But alas, monuments that lasted for centuries are now left in ruins or cannibalised in the name of civilisation. Such is true of the Benin Moat and City Wall. It seems we thrive at destroying all that we should hold dear.

I have often wondered when and where we lost it. It can't be because we are black; our forefathers were just as black with even less outside knowledge, but they preserved their cherished monuments. You see, by the time the colonialists departed our shores, they left us some monuments that they built with our money, of course. Some of these included the Governor General's house along Marina, the Race Course at Onikan, the Parliament House in Onikan, and the Independence Building also by the Race Course. There was also the Lord Lugard's House in Kaduna.

Just like the decay of some of our traditional structures, most of these 20th Century monuments are in various stages of dilapidation or have been transformed into new creations that provide little resemblance to or tell the story of their historical pasts. One such example is the present Tafawa Balewa Square (TBS) at Onikan. It occupies the position of the old Race Course that offered horse racing, cricket games, and leisure centres. As TBS, the place is now a concrete jungle of ubiquitous shops. I am not sure Sir Tafawa Balewa would have approved or felt honoured to lend his name to such hideous transformation. Years ago, the place was privatised following years of government mismanagement. The place is now best used to host the Lagos Trade Fair, Eyo Festival, and political rallies.

The independence building, a 25-storey structure was the first of its kind in Nigeria. It was both an administrative centre and a tourist sight for Lagos visitors. With the advent of military rule in Nigeria, it was eventually converted to the Ministry of Defense, who ran it aground until it was destroyed in a blazing inferno. It remains in its gutted state to date.

At Marina, metres away from the Independence building, is NECOM House, a 37-storey building that holds the international communication gateway for Nigeria and 13 other African countries. Built in the late 70s for and by NITEL, this tallest building in Africa was also gutted by fire in 1983. My companies, Costain (West Africa) Plc and Dolphin Properties Limited, renovated and managed it until it was privatised some years ago. I understand it has been sold again.

The Western Nigeria Television (WNTV) station, the first in Africa, was set up in Ibadan in 1959. By 1975, it was acquired by the newly owned Nigeria Television Authority (NTA), set up by the Federal Government. NTA today has not risen beyond the mouthpiece of the Federal Government, and that has stifled growth, development, and innovation.

We did not inherit everything from the colonialists; we built quite a lot ourselves, including infrastructures and businesses that should have been iconic and viable in themselves. Looking at the management failures of TBS and NECOM House, it should come as no surprise how our innovations ended up too. The National Theatre, which was built to host the major performances of Festac 77, gradually deteriorated to the point where just one cinema hall out of four was serviceable. In 2006, it was listed for privatisation.

In the early 70s, as part of the national economic development plans, the General Gowon Administration built six steel rolling mills in various parts of the country. These were meant to operate with steel billets from the Ajaokuta Steel Complex, then under construction by the Russians. Meanwhile, thousands of Nigerians had been given scholarships to study metallurgy, engineering, mining, geology, and the sciences in any university abroad that the students got admission. The Murtala Administration that came to power in 1976 sacked the so-called Super Permanent Secretaries (the drivers of this policy), suspended work on the Ajaokuta Steel Complex while placing it under a corruption probe, cancelled or delayed payments for some of the scholarships in progress. The nations steel industry, to this day, did not recover from this derailment. The steel rolling mills are dead, and the steel complex is comatose. As for the trained graduates, most of them relocated to Europe and the US after years of inadequate or no employment.

Similar stories exist with the three paper mills that were also established in the country in the 70s. Even our main economic stay, Petroleum resources have not been spared of the gross mismanagement that is the hallmark of self-governance in Nigeria. The major reason, if not the only one, why the petroleum refineries do not produce to capacity or near capacity, is because of Turn Around Maintenance (TAM), or lack of it. At their ages, and they had reached that threshold long ago, the TAM for each refinery has to be done yearly or less. I know this because Costain Oil & Gas part of the Costain Group to which my company, Costin (West Africa) Plc belonged, had a rolling contract for decades maintaining refineries in the Middle East. The planning and procurement for the next year's TAM begin the day the current one ends. That is because the refinery cannot be shut down for longer than three weeks. That is to say, you cannot carry out such operations on a “wait-for-contract-award" basis, a feature of Nigerian management.

At independence, Nigeria inherited the standard gauge railway network with four major nodes in Lagos, Port-Harcourt, Sokoto and Maiduguri. With the modest growth in commerce, we did not add to this network in any way until 2012-2016, that is, not counting what was done in preparation for Ajaokuta Steel Complex which was strictly to serve that complex. The effect was that the country relied mainly on road networks for the movement of goods and services. The roads were being constructed yearly, but with poor supervision, the quality of the end product was always unreliable. A second problem was our inexplicable practice of abandoning an old road network once a new one is built. We are supposed to be building to add, not to replace! Thirdly, as is the practice in all we do, the issue of maintenance of these roads is, perhaps, from all intent and purposes, never seriously discussed. We tend to believe that they would last forever. And fourth, we are not proactive in planning for road expansion, considering the population increase since independence and our reliance on road transportation. A second Onitsha Bridge over the

River Niger is still a phantom, more than ten years after it was first discussed.

One more sector worthy of mention here is the power sector. I have written a lot on this sector so I will not dwell so much on it here. It goes without saying that the country can never reach its potential until we get our power supply and distribution right.

Regrettably, the picture we present to the World is that of poor innovators and poor managers of what is ours. Africans are known to be proud people of their heritage. How then did we become comfortable with these derogatory labels? Nigerians make up 25 percent of the black population in the World. Our failure is the failure of the black race. Shall we allow this to continue?

Arts, Monuments, and Our Future: Beware, Says Our Future

In the last two parts of "Arts, Monuments, and Our Future", we looked at the travails of our ancient arts, as well as our pitiable attempts to maintain and manage the monuments that were handed down to us or built by us. I have chosen arts and monuments to portray this national malaise because these objects can be seen and are easily relatable. Nigerians are artistic in nature. Just listen to us talk, gesticulate, sing and dance. In central Lagos today as well as in Badagry, you will find vestiges of Brazilian and Portuguese Architecture. In the north, you will find the influence of Islamic or Arabian architecture. Do we have a Nigerian architecture? I do not know. But we do have Nigerian Art. Can we incorporate these into our architectural designs? Perhaps. It is important to leave our marks and history in our designs and the things we build; these will be our footprints. For a little more money, we can easily leave indelible forms in our iconic buildings and bridges. Today, the Lekki-Ikoyi bridge in Lagos is a must-shoot scene in every Nollywood movie, simply because of its design; a cable bridge, the first in Nigeria. We missed making such a statement with the Third Mainland Bridge, arguably the longest bridge in Africa. Shall we fail this time with the second Niger Bridge at Onitsha? You bet.

Holding on to what a people have and building new ones are great testaments of a civilised people. If we cannot do this, then, what kind of future are we going to have? It is said that there is no difference between the person that cannot read and the one that refuses to read. Both will remain ignorant. If we just build to replace, we have no future and no history to tell. The state of the power sector illustrates this quite well. If we didn't have the foreign investment in the telecommunication sector in 2000, we would still be battling with NITEL, its 200,000 landlines, and the "naught-nine-naught" (090) today.

Why are we like this? The answers are staring us in the face: corruption, poor education, near-zero patriotism, little or no manpower development, poor judiciary and accountability, stunted vision.

Corruption in the minds of many denotes fund embezzlement. Even our present Government operates on that premise. Corruption is far worse than that. Corruption is in nepotism, tribalism, justice denied, poor wages, project implementation, inaccurate billing, inadequate service provision, etc. When we employ the wrong candidate for a job, that is corruption.

During my primary school days, one of the subjects we were taught from primary five to six was civics. This core subject teaches one about nationality, citizenship, the responsibility of a good citizen, the responsibility of the state to you, law agencies and cooperation with the law, taxation, and patriotism. I understand that civics was replaced with social studies or something of some dubious name and contents. What do they teach our children now? And how about Nigerian History? What truth is told to our students about our journey from independence, apart from names of governors and presidents? When you give the wrong education, you end up with a poorly prepared workforce.

In spite of the colossal amounts spent on education, there has been a grave assault on our education system from various fronts: From government ministers who think that the South is unnecessarily preoccupied with paper qualification, to poorly paid lecturers, and ill-equipped universities. The Federal Government, with the so-called unity schools in every state, have also been in the business of establishing tertiary institutions in all 36 states of the federation. Though school enrollment figures are indeed on the rise, building more schools and universities is not always the solution. One can expand the existing universities and faculties to accommodate upwards of 30,000 to 50,000 graduations per university per session. The real problem is that the government still sees education as a social service. Education cannot be a social service. If a country has to develop, it must invest in the development of citizens from youth; we are not doing that. In real values, the budget allocation to education has not kept pace with technological growth and the requirements of the education sector in the 21st century. The federal government has to realise they do not have the resources to continue this way, and thus, must look at allowing the universities especially, to charge commercial fees adjusted with the level of subsidies they get from the government.

The Nigerian perception and attitude to public service work is that of "government work no be my Papa work." What this means is that the employees are not committed to producing results that they can be proud of; there is no zeal for excellence. A concoction of poorly educated workforce lacking the drive for excellence is a recipe for abject failure, and that is what we have. Our public servants do not understand that the only difference between public service and the private sector lies on the fact that the former is funded by tax-prayers and the later by private financing from investing individuals that founded each company. Beyond these differences in their genesis, they both need to have good corporate governance, operate profitably to remain viable, develop human resources, provide values to the macroeconomy, and take care of their employees. In other words, even social services are not meant to lose money or be wasteful. If we understand this, we just might be able to reverse our current destructive course.

Democracy can only thrive where and when the rule of law exists. By the rule of law, I mean all citizens must be equal in the eyes of the law and everyone is entitled to obtaining justice as a right. It is only under such social justice that everyone must be held accountable for their actions. In such a land, you can sue and be sued to redress infractions of the law. So must also be entities, institutions, and anyone or any business that provides any service. If there is no accountability, there will be no excellence in service. Since the advent of the military into our politics, the slogan has been to clean up the polity or fight against corruption. The first step in doing this is to establish the rule of law.

Sometime in the middle 90s, I took a trip to the Iponrin Telephone Exchange of NITEL in Lagos, to inquire on the reason we, in Costain (West Africa) Plc, were having no dial tones on our over ten landlines then. I was first given a tour of the installations, where I was shown the telephone circuits for all areas served by the exchange. In the process, they showed me the battery banks that were meant to power these circuits. The voltage meter on the monitoring console was reading zero.

My guide then took me to their power room. Of course, there was no power from PHCN then, and the 500kva generator there was quiet. Why? There was no diesel to power the emergency generator. Why? I asked again. My guide then took me to his office and showed me his revenue report for the last month. The exchange generated N84million (Naira) in that month and remitted all to Abuja. So, why would you not have diesel to power your generator? I asked incredulously. He replied that every month he had to apply for money for things like that, and it would take some time before he received a response of any kind. Whilst he is waiting, businesses are unable to run efficiently, and he is losing revenue, which the same people in Abuja expect him to improve upon.

This story illustrates the need for decentralisation. This is true of our national discuss today. We all look for a happy, hopeful, future, but know you this; we are the ones to create that future. Much harm has been done to our institutions, our monuments, infrastructure, our arts, and ultimately our history. Without history, we have no future. If we continue on the part of revisionism, we will have no future. We are not teaching our grandchildren right at the moment, and we have already misled our children enough.

In summary, after decades of misrule, our economic system has become laxer, and spasms of renascent losses are a sign of its shameful decline. We must make haste to put a stop to these losses; the implications of its continuity far exceed the imaginations of the absurdist artist. "Beware, the losses are too great," says the future.

PART VIII
THE RESONATORS

"Wisdom stands at the turn in the road and calls upon us publicly, but we consider it false and despise its adherents."

— Khalil Gibran

The Haves and The Have Nots: The Dangerously Widening Gap

The values of a nation influence what institutions are formed and how they perform. It is challenging to maintain a democracy if the underlying values necessary to sustain it aren't respected in the first place. When a nation fosters an acceptable form of democracy of knowledgeable, empathic, and analytical individuals to service the various institutions of power, there is real freedom for all. This country has all the structures available to thrive and be organised, and for "everyone" to freely choose their own path to succeed in the system; having good infrastructure and safety as a "right" rather than as a thing to "earn" or be "deprived." This is compatible with common sense, for when we are free of unbridled suffering, our brains become capable of being part of a socially complex society with self-control and a desire to be patriotic, to develop self as an individual and work for the benefit of others, not just self. But here, is chaos organised so intelligently that the order benefits only a select few, while the citizenry slave to get that which only ends up an illusion of what is rightfully theirs. Like a ticking time-bomb, the gap is tipping to the cusp of a dangerous outcome. In good governance, everyone benefits adequately, and only then, and then alone, can we achieve lasting peace and a thriving nation.

These were the thoughts going through my mind on this memorable day, June 12, 2019, as I turned up the television volume to listen to the President's speech. Thus, you can imagine my pleasant and somewhat, sceptical surprise hearing the President acknowledge the gap between the rich and the poor in the nation. It was very gratifying to note that Mr. President and I were thinking alike. It must be because of our age bracket that affords us the luxury of knowing by experience that there was a time when the gap wasn't so wide. He made this clear when he talked about having the privilege of free education from primary school to staff college and war college. He also received some of his education in England, India and the United States.

By addressing the gap, he simply identified the presence of a large population of Nigerians living in poverty and promised to lift the 100+ million of them from poverty in 10 years. I should add here that he only has four more years constitutionally; if his plan will take 10 to 15 years what's the guarantee that subsequent governments will follow through. Nigeria is a country where successors do not continue the good work of their predecessors.

I am eager to see the working plan and the implementation details of this plausible goal with the hope that it will not go down the drain as yet another one of those pronouncements we've had in the past with little or no execution road map. I will like to call on Mr. President to give us a clear road map of where we are, where he is planning to take us to, and how to get there. One that doesn't only include the social intervention programmes which he claims are a model for other nations. It is certainly a good idea to provide millions of school children with free meals in primary school; I can't say the same for the conditional cash support programme that gives N5000 to the poor. That will only give them daily bread for the moment, but no one is leaving the poverty bracket that way.

Mr. President will have to do more starting with looking back a little bit to why the six steel rolling mills, the six assembly plants, the refineries and paper mills that consumed billions of money were never fully utilised. If we can find an answer to these questions, maybe half of the 100 million would be lifted out of poverty. The secondary industries and the value chain from those industries were meant to give Nigeria the industrial take off at that time and provide millions of employments.

I had high expectations listening to the president because I felt he'd had enough time to prepare a speech that was scant on rhetorics and rich with policy and program specifics seeing how he kept the May 29 inauguration ceremony short by saying nothing.

I should add that this piece wasn't supposed to be about the President, well, not specifically. It was to address the fact that Nigeria was a country of a few "Haves," and many "Have-Nots." According to Oxfam, the international aid agency, Nigeria came in last or first depending on how you view it amongst countries fueling the gap between the super-rich and the poor. This was explained to be due to a "shamefully low" social spending, poor tax collection, and rising labour rights violation, among other things.

Back in the good old days in Nigeria, it was the norm that those who had extended their knowledge and wealth to mentor those that did not have, who then gradually grew, because the system allowed for such growth. Some of the Mentors include the Dantatas in the North, through trade and commerce; the Ojukwus in the East, through transportation, and the Odutolas in the West, through manufacturing. Amongst these Mentors were also top executives in the private sector. And individuals in the Customs and Police force, although, the general opinion then was that their source of wealth was questionable and not to be respected.

With the Nigerian Civil War ending in the 70s came the "cheap money syndrome" in the form of politicians in uniform and Agbadas with a winner take all mentality. At this stage, the gap between the haves and the have-nots started to develop. I recall something that happened at a social event where a retired school teacher was introduced and invited to the high table because way back then he taught those that had risen to become Professors and Generals. Today, teachers are on the bottom line of poverty.

As the gap widened, the haves started removing themselves and seeking special protection from the have-nots. They sought the protection of the security, the judiciary, and even the executive arm of government. The average Nigerian could not afford to be protected, and so becomes easy prey to mischief makers. Many were also unable to get justice because the lawmakers no longer followed the law.

Equity was replaced with quota, and then came marginalisation. It became very easy for those wanting to destabilise the country to find willing and able volunteers.

I can take you back to the origin of militancy in the South-South, the Boko haram insurgency, the Oduduwa, IPOB, and more but I'll spare you the details here, I will, however, state that if the present situation continues, there is no way our security organization can cope; after all, 80 percent of them are too busy protecting the haves, day and night. The hallmark of a successful nation is protection to everyone - the good, the bad, the rich, and the poor.

Let's take a moment to simply take in the number that now protects the presidency, almost all the legislators, the judiciary, the local government Chairmen and Counselors, the state government, and almost all the government functionaries, the heads of parastatals, the private sector heads, the traditional heads, and many former heads of something or nothing. We have not been able to stop and think, why are we protecting all these men and women? Who are we protecting them from and why?

The truth is that until the haves no longer fears the have-nots, society remains unsafe. However, the only way this can happen is if the have-nots no longer feel marginalised by the haves. Like a town crier, I sound the gong: If the gap isn't addressed swiftly with more than free food and N5000, a time is coming when the have-nots will have nothing else to eat but the haves. This is a stage worse than war because it will consume all of us - the haves, the poor, and the custodians of law and justice.

Beggars and Givers

The 2017 Christmas approached with the usual festive activities in full swing; hampers were sold in almost every shop, and also hawked on the streets with all kinds of Christmas commodities. The hampers and other Christmas goodies were dangled across peoples' faces to attract the usual buyers. On one fateful day, to avoid the insane rush that usually happens when it gets closer to Christmas day, my son, Chukwuemeka, decided to shop early at a particular shop along Adeola Odeku in Victoria Island. As he came out of the store, a responsible looking gentleman approached him. This gentleman, so well-spoken, told my son his life story of how he had been made redundant from his workplace and his four months' salary and benefits not paid, and the Christmas was approaching with a wife and two children to cater for, and some bills to pay. Hence, he needed a one-off help to settle bills till he got another job or something to do. All this he said close to tears that almost made my son join in the teary affair.

In a bid to help, my son, who felt the cash he had was not enough, went across to the ATM to withdraw some more money for the gentleman, while he waited. The "man in need" was eternally grateful. My son had remembered a proverb I once referred to that "if you give what you can afford, it is gracious, but if you give what you need, it's a novelty." So that day, he went home feeling very good but couldn't even tell his wife because at the time they were under immense financial trouble.

Less than ten days later, a day before Christmas to be precise, he came to visit me a few kilometres from where this gentleman had initially approached him; you can imagine his surprise when he ran into the gentleman again. At first, when he saw the gentleman approaching, he thought he was coming to show gratitude for the earlier help he had rendered. To his shock, the gentlemen didn't even recognise him, but instead proceeded to repeat the same pathetic story. So, who is the beggar, and who is the giver?

Sometime ago I listened to the former Minister of Agriculture, now President of the African

Development Bank, Adewunmi Adesina, being interviewed on CNN and he made a very clear point that the continent of Africa, particularly Nigeria, is not poor. It is the people that are poor. He went further to explain that there cannot be this much poverty in a continent that is endowed with so many resources - Metal, Iron, Clay, Gas, Oil, Cocoa, just to mention a few, as well as human resources.

I have often wondered, at what stage in a person's life does he or she get to and can convince himself or herself that the only way to survive is to beg. Some may argue that begging stems from poverty or disability; I beg to differ though, because the man we recently celebrated on June 12, the President we never had, Chief M.K.O. Abiola came from abject poverty. Stories of him reveal that he laboured in the day and played in a band at night to educate himself. And when he became very successful in business, he was able to identify with every class because he had seen it all; the poor, the middle class and high class were able to identify with him, which was why when he decided to contest for the Presidency, people of all classes, regardless of religion voted him into power.

When you travel the continent of Africa, you experience different categories of beggars. Some as a result of disability, some by the roadside performing and entertaining; however, some, I believe go with the notion that they are more likely to make more money from begging than engaging themselves in some meaningful form of labour, like the gentleman who approached my son.

I have worked as a volunteer in a school for the disabled and physically challenged, particularly blind men and women, and over the years I have seen many of them become Lawyers, Engineers, Mathematicians, Musicians, Teachers, etc., and in all my years as a volunteer, I have never known any single one of them preferring to beg before or after their graduation. Thus, it makes me wonder at what time in life do we engage in begging. How can someone put a child through the act of begging, no matter the cultural, traditional or religious connotation that goes with such an act? How safe are we when security men and women who guard our airports, churches, mosques, hotels, shopping centres, highways, etc., resort to begging, sometimes with guns in hand? The latter, an act that has become endemic to our society.

Now, the Givers:

The culture of begging can only exist with givers. Thus, to the givers let me first recite an old Chinese proverb, "You give a poor man fish, and you feed him for a day. You teach him to fish, and you give him an occupation that will feed him for a lifetime." This proverb simply means it is more worthwhile to teach someone to do something for themselves than do it for them on an ongoing basis. In as much as it is understood that there is a religious and cultural connotation that evokes a sense of giving, permit me to quote the Bible from Deuteronomy 15:10, *"Give generously to them and do so without a grudging heart; then because of this the LORD your God will bless you in all your work and in everything you put your hand to."* The Quran also places a huge emphasis on giving; in fact, it is an obligation and command on the Muslim to do so. The Quran repeatedly commands the Muslims to give Zakat, which you can essentially call a charity tax. One of the verses I can remember from the Quran (2:43) says, *"And be steadfast in prayer; practice regular charity; and bow down your heads with those who bow down."*

However, the Quran also forbids the Muslims from doing this generous act just so he can be praised, from (4:38), *"Not those who spend of their substance, to be seen of men, but have no faith in Allah and the Last Day: If any take the Evil One for their intimate, what a dreadful intimate he is!"* So, the Quran condemns those who give charity just so that it can be seen by everyone else, just so they can show off to everybody for their own big ego; the Quran is totally against this and wants Muslims to give charity out of pure sincerity! There have been several cases of people who have acquired funds from illicit ways only to have them give generously to Churches like the case of an army officer who defrauded the Bayelsa state government to the tune of N150 million and then gave N11 million to Winner's Chapel as offering. And the case of Lawrence Agada who worked in Sheraton Hotel, committed fraud and then funded a series of church projects in Christ Embassy. So, let us not be fooled by those who give so generously as their generosity may not be sincere. My son soon learned the hard way that what he had taught was generosity and sincere giving ended up from a grudging heart: Once he found out he had been scammed; he regretted his act of generosity. If one gives sincerely, there will never be a need to be resentful no matter the wrong one discovers later; one will simply smile and move on, after all you gave it freely.

Importantly, we must understand that there are two kinds of giving and both yield different results. There is the giving that empowers; herein, you lift and give a person the power to feed himself for a lifetime, thereby taking one more person off the street and making society a better place. Then, there is the giving that enables; herein, you fuel the person to remain comfortable in mediocrity and keep receiving hand-outs to feed him for a day, adding no value to both the individual and the society. I am a man who abides by several doctrines, and I believe it is very important to help the needy, as both the Quran and the Bible teaches. However, money is not the only way to help the needy; you can help teach them a skill by giving them your time; you can help them find some type of gainful employment; you can help a child through school; you can give back to the environment by planting a tree, or even by cleaning up your environment.

So, givers, I ask, are you giving to empower or giving to enable?

Without History

America, a place commonly referred to as the greatest nation on earth despite being a relatively young country of barely 200 years old, is full of people intensely proud of its history. A history that begun long before America became a united nation and continues to bind more than divide the people. I have always believed that history is important because it helps us understand the past to predict the future, thereby enabling us to create the future we want. It also allows us to avoid repeating the mistakes of the past over and over again.

Several schools of thought have it that the past helps a child understand who he or she is. So, it's not surprising that many young people today cannot relate to being Nigerians because they were never introduced to the past. Nigeria has yet to embrace her history and the people who played significant roles in it. Our ignorance of the past is not the result of a lack of information, but of indifference; we do not believe that history matters. But history does matter. It has been said that he who controls the past controls the future. Our view of history shapes the way we view the present, and therefore, it dictates what answers we offer for existing problems. Problems like ethnic unrest, territorial disputes, and religious wars can be closer to being solved if the origin of such unease were adequately understood.

We have learnt through the excavation of the Nok culture, Benin mask, Ife bronze, and many more relics of the past that "Nigeria" is over two thousand years old. Centuries ago, before it became a nation, the geographical space housed thousands of different tribes and cultures existing as separate entities with unique systems. Due to colonialism, those many tribes and cultures were forced to carry one flag and claim one nation. Yet, if only we could understand what made each tribe thrive as an entity, we could better begin to appreciate how that uniqueness can be a strength.

Now, fast forward to our post-colonial days; we have stories of great artists who used different mediums to express our way of life. Sadly, they are now only great outside the shores of their own country. Picasso famously said that African arts, particularly Nigeria, influenced his works, yet many will disregard our art for the foreign. Ben Enwonwu, the renowned Nigerian painter and sculptor, was arguably the most influential African artist of the 20th century. Only recently, his work sold for 1.8 million pounds in London. Similarly, the works of Oshinowo, Erhabor Emokpae, Bruce Onobrakpeya, and Yusuf Grillo are now being auctioned outside the country. While this is good news and exciting to many Nigerians, as it shows that our artists are finally getting the right recognition for their works, it is clear that there's still much work to do. Not too long ago, Picasso's work was found in a building site and sold in an auction for over 42 million pounds, also in London. As someone who has always been an admirer of Ben's work, I find it sad that when I converse with many young and not so young people, even art enthusiast, he is unknown to them. When they teach about art in schools and the people who shaped Nigerian art, what exactly do they talk about?

I recently visited the British Museum, which I have done many times, but on this occasion, as I was taken on a tour, I was told of an incident that occurred during the 51st Ooni of Ife, Oba Adeyeye Enitan Ogunwusi Ojaja's visit to the museum. You see, the British Museum is a treasure of historical works; a number of these works came from Nigeria. They are beautifully displayed and well represented. One of such works is the original gate of the Palace's Shrine that was taken many decades ago with the permission of the then Ooni of Ife and replaced with a golden gate by the British. The golden gate is still there as the entrance to the shrine till now. After seeing the original gate displayed at the British Museum during his visit, the present Ooni of Ife was said to have joked that the museum should take back their golden gate and return the original gate to the Palace.

I saw the humour in the Ooni's story, but it also made me think that we really need to start appreciating and respecting what we have and stop waiting for the outside world to do it for us. This can start with our elections; each election year we cast our votes; it will help to choose candidates that will not repeat history but pave the way to a new era that benefits us all. However, we can only make informed decisions with proper information. Part of the reason for this blatant disregard of very important symbols of nationality is the elimination of History from the curriculum in our schools (I'm aware it is being re-introduced into the curriculum; it's long overdue).

Nigerian stories have to be told to the younger generation so they can have an idea where we got it wrong, and we can give them a chance not to repeat the same mistake. We have many pre-independence and post-independence stories that can shed light on the Nigerian State, some of which include, the First Republic, the Military Era, the incessant coups, and how we became a democratic nation. These stories should not be swept under the rug, never to be heard again, for the sake of history not repeating itself. The educational value of all these to the younger generation must not be underestimated.

The Nation's Pride In Rot: Apapa Ports

The majority of cars and foreign products that we find in Nigeria come to us by way of the sea transportation system. The seaports are the backbone of movement of goods and services in the country and throughout the world. Like most infrastructure systems in the country, the Apapa ports are fraught with gross deficiency, and the ever-increasing demand challenges the network of roads and bridges, but even worse, is the excessive load and outright abuse of these infrastructures, as trucks, tankers, and people continue to push the limits of the existing bridge and roads leading to the ports.

In 1967, I had just returned from the United Kingdom, where I had gone to for study leave. On my return, my employer, the then Federal Ministry of Works posted me to take charge of the geotechnical works for the foundation of the Apapa-Ijora Bridge. It was one of the biggest projects the ministry was embarking on at that time. Most of the funding was from the World Bank, and they were actively involved in the construction of the bridge. In my role overseeing the geotechnical works, I was to report to a World Bank representative named Engineer Coleman. Engineer Coleman was a stickler for the rules and had very little tolerance for any level of unprofessionalism. I recall almost getting fired by him for being absent from the project site for a few hours. In my defence, as a young man fending for himself without any family support, my salary meant a lot to me, so when it was held back due to some administrative delay, I was desperate. Thus, in my desperation this fateful day, I had gone to the headquarters of the ministry to follow up on the status of my unpaid three months' salary.

I was probably gone for two to three hours but when I returned, I was met with a very upset project manager. Mr. Coleman's anger was that the foundation works of "any" construction were very critical, talk less of a project that meant so much to the country. He was of the opinion that I needed to keep an eye on things at all times, taking records of every excavation and filling that was taking place. I tried to explain my plight to him, but he didn't want to know about my unpaid salary because according to him, it was somebody's responsibility to follow up on that just as it was my responsibility to be on the project site at a specific time. So, he recommended me to be disciplined. This would have happened but for the timely intervention of Alhaji Sule Katagun, the then Chairman of the Public Service Commission.

As Mr. Coleman went on to explain, the Apapa-Ijora bridge construction was a very important project that had potentials to contribute hugely to the economy of Nigeria. Years later, his words still ring true, as the Ijora bridge is one of the only two major routes to Apapa ports, which are the busiest seaports in Nigeria.

Although I eventually resigned, quite dramatically, from the ministry, I was proud of the completion of the bridge, which turned out to be a road work and bridge work to behold; mostly due to Mr. Coleman's 'wahala', I must say. This was well over fifty years ago. But for the meticulous engineering works that were carried out by men of the then Federal Ministry of Works and the World Bank representative, we would have nothing left now. Little or no thanks to the abysmal maintenance culture of public infrastructure in the country.

In recent times, one Sunday afternoon, I decided to take a drive to Apapa where most of my early memories as a working adult were made. A journey that would usually take me no more than an hour on a bad day, which Sunday afternoon shouldn't be, took me no less than four hours. The once glorious Apapa has degenerated into a state of public shame characterized by its collapsed and collapsing roads, intractable gridlock, and the near stationary presence of trucks and tankers that have become the bane of the city. There is also the issue of bribery between tanker drivers and security personnel who are supposed to attempt restoring some level of orderliness in the region but would rather use the disorder to benefit their pockets. How? A tipping tanker driver gets to drive through faster than non-complaint tanker drivers. These qualities make Apapa's current state the perfect recipe for disaster waiting to happen.

As someone who has spent most of his life building roads and bridges, I know for a fact that no road or bridge in the world is designed to take this type of load in this manner. When constructing roads of this grade, you take into consideration the load-bearing capacity of the road; that is, you consider the potential load the bridge or road might need to bear at its highest peak. However, most of this consideration in designing the foundation and laying the surface work is mostly based on "the loads" continually moving, not permanently stationed for weeks and months on the roads or bridges. That is what a parking lot or terminal is for, not a bridge. If something is not done to remove the tankers from the bridges and roads quickly, those bridges will collapse in a few years.

Apapa was one of the most beautiful places to reside in Lagos; many notable people lived there, like Gen. Murtala Mohammed before Dodan Barracks, Gen. Ike Nwachukwu, Admiral Ndubisi Kanu, and many more. I remember correctly that a lot of Nigerian Port Authorities and Navy personnel lived there; I know this because I was also a resident of Apapa. Today, many of us cannot see any residue of the Apapa we once knew. I doubt any Lieutenant Colonel in the army will be quick to take up accommodation in Apapa.

As an environmentalist, I am quick to spot the fact that the current state of that city is prime for a number of hazardous practices like public unsanitary disposal of human waste, with tanker drivers sleeping in their vehicle for days without access to any toilets; thus, canals and roadsides become the dumping ground. We also will have massive littering of waste as small traders migrate to where there is the likelihood of business, and in most cases, they don't travel with trash cans or bags, not when the ground is available to welcome their waste and that of their customers. Then, there is the security implication of tired, and sometimes, angry people waiting for days with little or no rest. Some, sometimes, resort to drugs and alcohol for the energy to survive the long journey that they will still embark on after leaving Apapa with the goods for delivery.

Ports are meant to support and benefit local, state and federal economies through their role in creating jobs and transporting goods. They also serve as a significant resource for national defence and emergency preparedness. The current state of Nigeria's seaports is in no shape to achieve these goals effectively; neither is it primed for export diversification nor stable foreign exchange earnings because they are seriously deficient. We must understand the critical role of ports to help us more effectively engage with decisions that impact near-port communities. The situation in the port city of Apapa and its environs cannot improve if the deficient ports are not addressed. However, not only will Apapa and its environs suffer if the deficient seaports are not addressed, but the nation will also suffer an irreparable blow to the financial brain, as export and import activities, which we depend upon as a significant source of foreign exchange, will collapse. Even the oil we so heavily depend on will fail us, as it will lose the major inlet for the refined and outlet for the crude to service the nation's pocket.

According to the Nigerian Ports Authority (NPA), the country has six seaports: Apapa and Tin Can in Lagos State, the Onne and Port-Harcourt ports in Rivers State, the Warri port, and the Calabar port. But, by many accounts, only the Lagos ports are operating anywhere near full capacity. The persistent immobile heavyweights and high traffic on the Apapa-Ijora bridge mean increased potential for accidents and eventual collapse of the bridge that leads to the nation's functional port. We cannot afford to apply our usual lackadaisical response to issues to this rot; to do so will only spell doom for the nation.

Power Corrupts, Absolute Power Corrupts Absolutely

One quote that has always checked me over the years as I climbed the corporate ladder to the top of the construction chain was by Lord Acton, a British historian of the late 19th and early 20th centuries. It says, *"Power tends to corrupt, and absolute power corrupts absolutely."* Lord Acton believed that a person's sense of morality lessens as his or her power increases. This served as a note of warning to me, and I could either decide to prove Acton's belief right or wrong as I progressed in life. While I would like to say that I was able to prove Acton wrong, I can recall instances when having power threatened my morals, especially in Nigeria.

With frequent conversations around me on how elections are often conducted in Nigeria, I found myself thinking about power and how our leaders are a perfect example of Lord Acton's quote. We have come to almost accept that those in power often do not have the people's best interests in mind; they are primarily focused on their own benefits and may abuse their position of power to help themselves. In fact, if we surveyed the next crop of leaders, we may find that most of them are seeking power (in this case, political office) for the same reason of amassing wealth for their families and friends. This is the only kind of "leadership" we have come to know in recent decades.

I always caution myself against giving in to cynicism because that is not my way. However, I have seen in many cases how the slight resemblance of power given to an individual in any position of high or low ranking completely intoxicates the person to act out in total self-interest. From the policemen on the street, brandishing guns meant to protect as a tool of intimidation to exploit both the innocent and guilty, to drivers of top officials driving like maniacs and blasting sirens when alone in the car, only to stop on the way to buy roasted plantain; obviously, the siren and reckless driving were essential for the satisfaction of his craving for "Boli."

In Nigeria, sirens are a good way to point out abuse of power. My understanding of a siren is of a loud noise-making device typically used to warn of natural disasters or attacks or in emergencies; hence, the reason people respect the siren and give way when they hear it coming. However, we can all boldly say that it isn't often the case in our beloved nation. I recall an experience I shared in my autobiography about the power of the siren. During a Salah celebration some years back, I was in my village when a former minister friend rang me up to enquire about my whereabouts. I told him that I was simply relaxing in the village; he then mentioned that he was sending something across to me. At that time, I had no idea what it was, but I was soon to find out a few hours later in a most interesting way.

My village is very serene with barely any sound of vehicular traffic, and my house is tucked away far from the heart of town. All of a sudden, I could, hear the sound of a siren getting louder and louder until it was almost at my gate. My immediate thought was that my minister friend had come himself to deliver the gift. I went to the gate intending to receive whomever it might be.

When I got to the gate, I saw a Hilux pick-up van with a Ram at the back. It had two other occupants, the driver and an orderly. I was rattled and had to ask if they had been responsible for the siren, to which the orderly, who laid down flat to greet me, responded with, *"Oga, it is Sallah na."*

I couldn't get over it; the use of the siren in a former minister's vehicle when he was not in it. So, was the siren meant for the Ram?

This got me wondering about the use of sirens which naturally led me to ponder about the power dynamic that it appropriates, legitimises and perpetuates. The siren has always had to do with power. For information purpose, the siren was not invented in Nigeria or by a Nigerian, even though we love the sound of it. The siren has its origin in Greek mythology. It referred to a group of creatures who used to pose as beautiful women and then tempt hapless sailors with their lovely songs. Bewitched by the sonorous songs the sailors would usually crash their ships into the rocks and drown or be eaten by the creatures. Does this sound familiar?

Think of flashing lights as beguiling beauty, think of the blaring sirens sowing confusion in the minds of drivers, and then think of drivers crashing into each other as they try to make way for the loud sirens in their wake, and you can see clearly where it all came from.

So, these people ensconced close to power,

symbolised, in this instance, by the possession of a car fitted with blaring sirens, couldn't imagine not causing a ruckus even if it was just the driver and orderly in the car on a personal mission for their boss. I felt bad and was tempted to tell my friend about the incident, but I decided against it as I didn't want to ruin the young men's day; thus, I simply called him and expressed my gratitude for the gift.

Another way the average man or woman abuses power is through the use of uniforms. When people hear "power", they think immediately of position or an office, but power is a range of different things.

Growing up as a child in Akwukwu-Igbo, I came to the quick realisation that there was something powerful about uniforms, but I didn't fully comprehend what it was exactly until much later in life. But I could see even then that men or women in uniform always got plenty of attention. They did not just exude formality and officialdom, they also seemed to wield some sort of power, and it did not matter whether they were policemen or soldiers, court messengers or sanitary inspectors. Their uniforms seemed to transform and imbue them with power beyond the ordinary. Till date, put a man in uniform and watch him transform into something different, no matter whether he is guarding a bank, an embassy, or a fast food outlet.

If ordinary men with no position transform into self-serving individuals at the slight taste of power, do we have to wonder what they will do with even more power?

My fellow Nigerians, our leaders come from among us, the people, so the time has come for us to start demanding better from each other, be it in our offices, schools, or streets. Lawlessness shouldn't be condoned. Neither should greed, unprofessionalism, and mediocrity be tolerated. If we, the people, become better, we will never settle for leaders that have no real grasp of what leadership entails.

The change starts with each of us exercising our innate power to do better, and our patriotic power to go out and vote the right people into positions of power, each election year. Let's call out things that will compromise the process of a free and fair election. Let's be respectful, sensible, and orderly in using the power we have. Finally, let's be selfless with our choices in using the power others leave in our care.

The Songs from the Birds and the Dance Of the Trees

My favourite part of waking up early in the morning is listening to the birds chirping away amongst themselves in a language I may not understand, but I certainly enjoy. I often joke that when trees move, they must be dancing to the songs being sung by the birds and carried by the wind; it is music to my ears and a sight to behold. I am not always blessed with this early morning nature call when I'm in the city, which is why I spend most of my time lately outside the city. A good percentage of Nigerians like me that have populated the urban cities come from one village or local town around the country. But we so quickly forget the sounds of the early mornings and late evenings that come from hundreds of different birds that migrate in and migrate out of these communities and the dancing trees that move to the music of the birds, especially when there is enough wind.

There are people in my village that can interpret the meaning of the songs from almost all the birds. From the songs, they are often able to forecast weather changes, when to begin the planting and harvesting seasons, and even foretell the outcome of certain events. Although birds can sing at any time of the day; however, during the dawn chorus, their songs are often louder, livelier, and more frequent. Experts say the choir is mostly made up of male birds, attempting to attract mates and warn other males away from their territories. They are also convinced that the sounds are reassuring to humans because over thousands of years of evolution we've learned that the sweet melody of birds is an indication that our environment is safe. The trees, which serve as performance Stage for the birds, rustle and sway to the music as the wind caress' it; that union is such a beautiful thing to behold.

Sometimes, I am so intrigued that I just stand in awe of this graceful union. It doesn't stand rigid, resisting the flow of energy; it doesn't push back. These movements also supplement the wind pattern and arrival of rains, through the migration of these birds and other biodiversity. How can we forget so easily, and now live in cities with very few trees, shrubs, and grass? With each tree we cut down and refuse to replenish, we further alter the migration route of the birds, causing them to come less and less because there will be nowhere for them to perch. If we keep up with our idea of development that lacks sustainability: further replacement of natural habitats by artificial elements, such as houses, sand filling, and streets, leading to disturbances and negative impacts on different biological taxa, the little biodiversity we have remaining will migrate to other territories. Without these trees, forests and wetlands, our quality of life will continue to deteriorate.

The earth is designed to be sustained when all biodiversity is in sync; thus, the earth falls apart when the sync can no longer hold. Nature gave us everything, and in return, we have continued to abuse it. It's only common sense to know that whatever you abuse will someday fight back; nature is now fighting back. Nature was there before us, the inhabitants, because we needed it to survive, but over the years, we prefer to create our fake beaches, replace sand with concrete and artificial greenery. We even replace the actual sounds of birds, ocean, winds and trees with generator sounds and man-made audio sounds to be played in our concrete walls. You see those little islands in the pacific that was provided by nature for biodiversity as a stopover during migration have been taken over by man to build fancy cities, towns, and in some cases countries, for our pleasure without making proper provisions for the islands' original purpose.

The question is, don't we ever ask ourselves why certain things exist the way they do and what the consequences may be for altering them? Nature has a system, one that has worked for many centuries until we decided to disrupt that system. It is time we understand that man is not superior to its environment; the catastrophes that are emanating from the eye of the storm should serve as a wakeup call of our vulnerability. The hurricane, mudslides, floods, tornadoes, earthquakes that have inflicted the world are coming as a result of the pressure to which we have subjected the land and water.

With the massive agricultural development around the country, we must try not to over cultivate or overgraze the land. A proper system needs to be in place to monitor this, and not just a campaign encouraging more farming. The culture and method of shifting cultivation must be followed to allow the land to recover the needed nutrients.

In Lagos, the hunger for beachfront properties on the island has given rise to the act of sandfilling the ocean to create land, without developing proper gateways for the water to pass through. You can only push the water away for so long before it pushes back, especially when due to greed and sheer incompetence. We cannot continue to take so much from the land without replenishing.

For many people living in the cities, wildlife and nature is often something we watch on television. It is saddening that many have forgotten and can no longer hear the songs of the birds or see the dance of the trees. Maybe if we did, we would feel more connected to the very things keeping us alive and work harder to secure our survival by ensuring the preservation of our environment. The reality is that the air we breathe, the water we drink, and the food we eat all ultimately rely on biodiversity. Some examples are obvious: Without plants, there would be no oxygen, and without bees and other insects to pollinate, there would be no fruits and nuts.

www.ingramcontent.com/pod-product-compliance
Lightning Source LLC
Chambersburg PA
CBHW031144270326
41931CB00006B/141

9781946530219